ALL THUMBS

ALL THUMBS

MOBILE MARKETING
THAT WORKS

MICHAEL DRU KELLEY

First published in 2014 by
PALGRAVE MACMILLAN®
in the United States—a division of St. Martin's Press LLC,
175 Fifth Avenue, New York, NY 10010.

Where this book is distributed in the UK, Europe and the rest of the world,
this is by Palgrave Macmillan, a division of Macmillan Publishers Limited,
registered in England, company number 785998, of Houndmills,
Basingstoke, Hampshire RG21 6XS.

Palgrave Macmillan is the global academic imprint of the above companies
and has companies and representatives throughout the world.

Palgrave® and Macmillan® are registered trademarks in the United States,
the United Kingdom, Europe, and other countries.

ISBN: 978–1–137–27927–9

Library of Congress Cataloging-in-Publication Data

Kelley, Michael Dru.
    All thumbs : mobile marketing that works / Michael Dru Kelley.
      pages cm
    ISBN 978–1–137–27927–9 (hardback)
      1. Internet marketing. 2. Mobile commerce. 3. Branding (Marketing)
    4. Mobile communication systems. I. Title.

HF5415.1265.K392 2014
658.8'72—dc23   2014004352

A catalogue record of the book is available from the British Library.

Design by Newgen Knowledge Works (P) Ltd., Chennai, India.

First edition: August 2014

10 9 8 7 6 5 4 3 2 1

Printed in the United States of America.

CONTENTS

INTRODUCTION

The Focus and Goal
of *All Thumbs*

MY GOAL FOR *ALL THUMBS* IS TO DELIVER TO THE reader the experience and practical know-how I've attained as a seasoned marketing executive and entrepreneur. I have struggled, like many of you, with less knowledge, less time to market, and certainly less budget when making big decisions and needing big results. To keep things simple, here is what *All Thumbs* will focus on. With mobile devices reaching a penetration rate covering the vast majority of adult Americans and nearly half of the world's population, I will focus on the simple premise that marketers must make every piece of marketing mobile ready. Whether these are 30-second TV spots, radio ads, out-of-home, direct-mail pieces, newspaper ads, e-mail, in-store displays, or even online video, the mobile experiences we create must be easily activated with the press of a thumb and allow consumers to use a coupon, engage with a 90-second "how-to" video, or interact in any number of ways to drive sales of our brands, large and small.

As such, this book specifically focuses on a very simple yet practical way to help marketers—from small "mom-and-pop" organizations to multinationals, as well as those in different sectors and mobile literacy levels—build campaign-driven, mobile brand experiences that are designed for maximum effectiveness, yet are so efficient to create that they could be disposed of once a marketing campaign, even a very short one, ends. By campaign-driven, I mean that campaigns are typically defined as a single, short-term event or experience for a specific marketing effort that lasts for just a few hours around a big TV tent-pole event, or for the standard four to eight weeks around a coupon offer, product sample, product launch, or specific marketing push.

This book will not focus on mobile app design, responsive design trends, or tablet experiences, although I do think lessons can be learned from building mobile experiences for these platforms. Mobile seems very daunting to brands of every size because when you think mobile, you think about big app or web builds with massive costs, long development time frames, and product roadmaps from IT departments that would boggle most GPS systems. Mobile has also come on the scene so quickly that many in business are still ignorant to the capabilities, which I also hope to help change with *All Thumbs*. Much of this mobile activity seems out of the control of or out of reach for marketers and business owners, depriving the entire company of sales gains and marketing success.

There is a path forward that we will take together.

I have written *All Thumbs* as guidance for brands to achieve success building inexpensive, campaign-driven mobile experiences that they can easily fold into the budgets of existing, traditional marketing campaigns. Typically, I develop these experiences in mobile-optimized, common web language, such as HTML, that can be found in virtually every community. This is preferred to the complicated and lengthy processes of mobile applications or large-scale websites, which then need to be retrofitted for mobile.

Brands *can* make very small investments in campaign-driven mobile experiences, which can be "re-decorated" from campaign to campaign and baked into a company's overall, larger website and longer-term digital strategy, or even thrown out at the end of the campaign without the budgetary, operational, or technical pain that may come with app or web development. Most importantly, the campaign-driven mobile experiences can be tailored to specific objectives, returning a much higher return on investment (ROI) over the life of a marketing plan. No matter the size of your company, you can create a mobile marketing effort that is easy and inexpensive. I will tell you how and also where to leverage your existing marketing efforts that you know have been successful, but that you are now ready to take to a whole new level of engagement with the mobile device. In *All Thumbs*, I will provide some examples of mobile campaigns that I have both observed and been part of developing. In some cases, I have blinded the company or changed the variables, such as brand category, to help better illustrate the examples.

Finally, I end every chapter with a "Thumb's Up" series of tips to help summarize the key points for quick application as well as to provide a format to get your feedback. I want to hear your tips, too! Please provide your tips at allthumbsbook.com, and I will periodically share the best ideas with social networks and possibly include them in future editions of this book. We are just at the beginning of mobile marketing. I look forward to hearing from you on how we can move mobile marketing forward for maximum impact.

I hope *All Thumbs* guides your brand in kick-starting its mobile marketing and helps it evolve far beyond the lessons, tips, and examples I give in this book—so that in turn, I can learn from you. Here's to you being an inspired, driving force within your business, and an All Thumbs Expert.

CHAPTER 1

All Thumbs

The Simple Rule of Thumb
for Mobile Experiences

EVERYONE HAS A MOBILE PHONE, BUT
FEW KNOW MOBILE MARKETING

A few days before I embarked on writing this book, I met with a
Fortune 100 CEO and CMO. Both were tapping away on their
phones as the meeting started—a common scene in corporate
conference rooms across the globe—and they apologized, saying
that they needed a few minutes to respond to some urgent texts
and e-mails. I sat patiently and turned off my own phone, putting it safely in my coat pocket—a practice I have embraced as
common courtesy during meetings of any type. I watched them

as they both continued to tap at their devices. I observed that both were using their thumbs, and the CEO held up his index in a perpetual "just wait a minute" pose, almost forgetting he had done it. The CMO was alternating between two devices—a Blackberry and an Android. The CEO had three devices.

As I watched them for what felt like an eternity, I filled the time by observing how they used their phones. The fact that both were using thumbs to create messages, just as I do, made me realize that in the mobile world, most consumers are indeed "all thumbs." However, many business owners and executives managing brands also feel like they are "all thumbs"—meaning they feel very clumsy and ignorant when it comes to mobile marketing. In fact, as I began to think about a working title for this book, I thought, "Wait a minute, that's it!" And thus the title of the book as well as this first chapter were created as I sat there with these thumb-tapping executives.

I was daydreaming of the front cover graphics when the CEO looked up from his phone, and, to break the ice, I said, "Three mobile devices. Impressive." He smiled, looking down at the three mobile devices that he referred to as "soldiers" lined up in front of him. He fidgeted with each to get them perfectly aligned just like soldiers in a lineup, pointed to each, and said in turn, "Work, home, and girlfriend. . . . Just kidding on the last point," he said, smiling.

He continued: "OK, let's begin. The reason we asked you here is because we are told that you are an expert in mobile marketing and we know nothing about mobile marketing. Where should we begin?" This was a stunning question. I was sitting with two people who had five mobile devices between them and were very successful in marketing their business, but they were confused about where to begin with their own efforts in this medium.

.I took a deep breath as I always do when faced with such a common conundrum. "You have to ask yourselves, 'What experience, as a consumer, do I want from my brands on the mobile device?' Clearly, as consumers, you are very adept with your devices. Let's just start there. Think like a consumer, not like a CEO or CMO. What would your ideal consumer experience of the mobile screen be if you could draw it on a single sheet of paper for your target customer? How would you simplify it for them if they were in the store deciding between your brand and a competitor's brand, while watching your 30-second spots or seeing your billboards in an airport?" This launched us onto a much different discussion, and ultimately we decided on a very different strategy than the CMO or the company's executive team had contemplated or executed.

WITH MOBILE, IT STARTS WITH THE CONSUMER, NOT THE TECHNOLOGY

My advice to the executives, and to any brand owner creating mobile campaigns, is that you have to start with the consumer. You also have to include multiple functions within the company—marketing, finance, product, retail, etc.—to create an effective, consumer-focused experience for the smallest screens we have ever seen. However, we often make the mistake of fitting our consumer experience to the media instead of understanding how the mobile screen can bring to life the experience in new, never-contemplated ways. And, like any effective marketing campaign, a successful experience starts with understanding your customer and why they are attracted to your brand in the first place. When it comes to mobile marketing, forget about the cool new technology and go back to the basics of marketing—really understanding what consumers want. You have to become part entrepreneur, unencumbered by the past or current practices, business traditions, organizational structures, shortcuts for resource-constrained staff, or already approved media plans to build what your customers are looking for. This is a whole new mobile world, and you have to think in a whole new way.

Another of the inhibitors in these early days of developing good mobile experiences for marketing campaigns is blindly turning over a project to the IT department. The IT team is often overwhelmed with dozens of priorities; they are often understaffed and underfunded. While they mean well, they understandably don't know the target consumer as well as the brand managers or marketers do. It's become almost a reflexive move, but I have witnessed some of the biggest companies hand control of mobile-activated advertising campaigns to IT departments, who design them so that consumers go directly to the main website or a page within the site. While this practice may make sense and save time and money at the outset, web destinations are often not the proper scale or content to fit mobile screens, let alone tailored to the objectives of an individual marketing campaign or effort. Many brands are also adding apps to their mobile arsenal, which have become default destinations or downloads regardless of the marketing objectives of an individual campaign. But the point of this book is to focus on marketing campaigns, and very rarely are apps created for individual campaigns of short duration.

Another big disrupter in advancing mobile marketing is done by those who see a new opportunity and "land grab it" by calling it "digital." I dare say that mobile is hardly like the digital platforms of the past, simply based on screen size and functionality alone, and actually requires its own focus from development to budgets, management, execution, research, design, implementation, and ROI, which I will get into later in this book. Because of the lack of expertise in building and monitoring mobile-only experiences, digital teams tend to default to what they know—such as ad units and content for larger screens; expensive, time-consuming product road maps that boggle the mind; or a lazy, shortcut approach of sending someone to a part of the existing brand website that may appear to "check off" a marketing requirement established at the beginning of a campaign. But this hardly satisfies the consumers or, as a result, the marketing department during the campaign or at the end when ROI is being examined.

When it comes to mobile web experiences that support individual marketing campaigns, we are still very much in the early days. I sort of feel like I did in 1996 or 1997 at the advent of the first fully developed and functioning "website." Similarly, mobile marketing is in the early days of those flat, unsatisfying consumer experiences, where technologists are creating with little or no marketing expertise. As a further example, banner ads that work well with a larger computer screen are simply being retrofitted for much smaller mobile screens, regardless of impact to consumer experience and marketing effectiveness. Sure, everyone in the 1990s had a different view of what constituted a good web page. Come to think of it, many people—especially engineers—still think they know what it means to have a good web page for the average consumer, when in fact many don't. Good virtual design must involve marketing input, which will always put consumers first. The same goes for mobile experiences. Just because you have engineered some aspect of digital doesn't suddenly make you a mobile expert. Proximity does not equal capability. You have to carve a new path that puts the brand managers and marketers in the driver's seat. You need to put the consumer experience first and adapt new mobile technology to it.

Two companies I admire that have really started to talk to their target markets with effective mobile campaigns are Coca-Cola and Procter & Gamble. P&G started mobile activation for all of their print ads under the Gillette family of brands, which are aimed at young, adult males. It is clear that consumers are meant to use the scan codes, which are as large as any element in the ad, with their mobile devices. Wendy Clark, the Senior Vice President of Marketing for Coca-Cola, sums it up this way for Coke Zero, a product also aimed at a younger male demographic: "Mobile has got to be an integral part of every single campaign we undertake or we are missing a very big part of the conversation with our customers."

TAKE CONTROL OF THE EXPERIENCE

So, how do brand managers and marketers respond when their campaign objectives, voices, and consumer desires are lost?

Because the advancements we see in mobile devices are so staggering, technology departments in any company often lead the way in terms of testing, discovering, and trying new things with their budgets. This is why IT or some similar function initially has a guiding hand in developing mobile plans. However, many technologists will tell you that they do not fully understand nor do they want to have responsibility for the marketing experience. They would rather be in a position to support their marketing and brand peers in developing effective marketing campaigns— more of a role on *how* to do something rather than *what* to do.

The marketing team needs to preside over the marketing experiences. Thus, there is often a precedent for you to offer a swift and efficient solution that is controlled, created, and managed by the marketers and supported by those in technology. Today, and with increasing advancement and availability, websites are being built specifically for mobile functionality that are far less expensive and time consuming alternatives to what has been created to date. Creating a mobile-optimized website also allows you to support an individual marketing campaign by mixing together different parts of the brand's overall web presence, apps for different functionality, and external assets, such as branded videos and music on places like YouTube and in the iTunes store. Sometimes these parts exist and can be brought together quickly and easily, and they can be constructed to work on multiple mobile devices. Sometimes you need to build web features to support the campaign or business objectives. These do not have to be expensive, and they can even have a shelf life that extends to future campaigns or even extends to become part of the brand's permanent website.

One of the most abused terms regarding visual and functioning experience is "mobile optimization, or, I think it is." You will often hear people say, "Our website is mobile optimized" or, "We built this beautiful site, but didn't have the budget to optimize it for mobile." (By the way, I'm not sure which is the more frustrating statement.) Regardless, "mobile optimization" is thrown around because many know that ignorant, non–mobile savvy executives—which many will claim to be—have no idea or any experience with what *mobile optimization* really is. Many executives assume their sites are optimized without really trying for themselves—as consumers. Worse yet, they blindly repeat "mobile optimization" to their bosses, peers, analysts, and boards, hoping that—until now—no one calls them out on it.

WHAT IS MOBILE OPTIMIZATION ANYWAY?

So how does one truly define mobile optimization? Let's answer by first looking at steps you can take to assess your brand's presence on mobile. When I start working with a brand, I check out every facet of their virtual presence—social, mobile, online, etc.—through my own personal mobile device. This is an easy, and often overlooked, place to begin. By checking out the websites on mobile, you immediately see if the functions and designs work well for a small screen. And by following a brand's social pages, you start to see if the personality of posts and the features offered are both in line with the brand positioning as well as effective for mobile devices. If you don't like the mobile experience that others have said is good, then it's very likely your target consumers won't either. The damage caused by an effort that was tested and failed is one thing; the damage caused by not testing a mobile experience at all is inexcusable. You would not believe the number of mobile-activated print and TV ads that were not tested first. One recent example was a consumer good aimed at the demographic of men between the ages of 18 and 25. The marketing effort performed well on computer screens, but did not function on mobile despite the extremely high penetration and usage of mobile within this target audience. As it turns out, no one tested the experience! Everyone, from the lowest to highest levels of your company, should test every experience as a consumer before going live.

Next, you have to experience your brand on a wide variety of mobile devices—not just your favorite personal device. There is no way to call your brand's experience optimal if it only works on a few devices or only one type of device. Like most consumers, I often sit in front of my TV with a computer, tablet, and phone within easy reach. Depending on my mood or energy level, I will text on my phone. Other times, if I am far behind on e-mail, I'll grab my laptop because I can punch out about 95 words a minute. For me personally, touch screens on phones can't compare when I need to be this productive. Then, there are other times when I grab the tablet to read or watch several news outlets while I watch several other news outlets on my TV.

You can never predict how or where the consumer will interact with your brand, so you have to optimize the experience for every device. Because a majority of people will likely engage with your brand's mobile strategies on a mobile device, you obviously have to understand what your brand's mobile experience is across a number of screens. Also, social sharing means that the consumer has just fractured the experience across a landscape of different devices—another reason why seamless functioning is important whenever or however I access a brand's mobile experience.

The tactic I employ to test a brand's mobile experience on multiple devices is simple and available to all of us on nearly every street corner. It's also full proof that I am testing it on the very latest devices available today and covering a majority of the consumer market. I simply walk into a Verizon or AT&T store and look at the brand's web, social, and mobile presence through a variety of screens and devices. If you are in any way responsible for the management of a brand and have never done this, I urge you to cancel today's lunch and try it; better yet, order a sandwich to go with your lunch date and do it together. It is likely you will be shocked or even horrified at the results. While you may think your brand's experience is optimal on your own personal iPhone or Android, which typically represents the enterprise's choice for mobile phones, you should be noting how suboptimal it often is on different mobile devices, tablets, and other devices, including computers. Don't delude yourself with facts and figures. You do not have an optimal mobile experience if it does not look as intended or function well on 90 percent of devices out there. However, optimizing it is not as tough or expensive as it sounds (I will discuss this later in the book). You just need to find the resources that are committed and experienced, which you will be surprised to know already reside in your company, ad agency, or other service provider.

So, when creating the experience how do we ensure it's optimal? When creating the user experience for a major health insurer to support the mobile activation of its 30-second spots during the Olympics, I found the number of experiences and potential screens confusing. So, like writing a recipe for an elaborate dish, I broke down each step of the consumer experience in sequential order, illustrated with the sketch of the mobile screen for each step. This step-by-step visual depiction of the consumer experience or "recipe" helped everyone involved, from the developers to the agency reps to the brand managers, understand how the consumer would flow through the mobile experience. It helped us to make adjustments, simplify the flow, and eliminate a number of mobile screens while keeping the experience focused on the objectives of the campaign.

You would also be surprised how often I see designs from the most established brands not fitting the mobile phone screens properly. In other cases, I have seen mobile web experiences for one type of phone—say, the iPhone—look terrible on other phones. Clearly brands have not provided the time, budget, or resources to design for all the other devices that make up the rest of the smartphone market. Whether the screen design is crowded, which causes the user to have to employ significant hand movements to navigate, or does not work well on other devices, abandon rates will climb, in some cases above 90 percent. When the screen is not designed properly for the majority of phone devices, you will often see 100 percent abandon rates. Another troubling issue is that sometimes brands create a mobile experience with links that lead to dead ends or the wrong pages. Yes, dead ends with no way back! Trust me, no one likes your brand so much that they would return after reaching a dead end or wrong page.

So, focus on the visual experience is paramount. First, I believe in absolute simplicity. The visual design should be limited to no more than a few actions for the consumer to take. My rule of thumb is typically limited to three main actions. Sure, each one can lead to more, but it's best to keep each screen focused with a design that gives room to breathe and be easily seen. Too many features will typically lead to a crowded, unreadable design that will confuse consumers, leading to high abandonment rates. Each screen should only have two or three features, and each feature should have no more than four words and one associated visual to tell the user what the feature is. This will greatly enhance consumer engagement and comprehension.

DEXTERITY AND DESIGN ON MOBILE IS ALL ABOUT THE "THUMBS"

Dexterity is a key factor. Navigation of an optimal mobile experience begins with the thumbs. We are now using a new technology that could literally evolve the human species over the next several generations. It has long been viewed that what makes us different from other mammals is that we have opposable thumbs. That said, I could see further evolution due to mobile use with finger joints changing, peripheral vision expanding, and overall eyesight either strengthening or worsening depending on genetics. In any case, most people that I've observed navigating mobile experiences—either apps or mobile websites—prefer to use their thumbs. Increasingly, we are seeing responsive design and mobile-built sites employing simple ladder layouts to make scrolling navigation more commonplace than tapping. Users typically scroll down with the thumb, while those who tap employ all fingers.

Carolyn Everson, who runs Facebook's global marketing solutions and sales, tells me that the "thumb" philosophy is a primary focus of the consumer experience. "Facebook is focused on 'thumb friendly' and 'thumb stopping' executions. We know it's all about engaging the consumer and the experiences have to be easily navigated with the thumb and be able to stop in an instant, again with the thumb. We use these terms every day when advising our brand partners."

Since a majority of smartphones increasingly have touch-screen functionality, most of us will often move our bodies in some way and use the phones at the same time. I believe you shouldn't move and use your phone—whether you're driving, walking, biking, skiing, or even picking up a cup of coffee. I can't begin to tell you how many minor household accidents I have caused and then wasted valuable time cleaning up because I was talking on or using my mobile phone at the same time.

However, human nature is human nature. We are all multi-tasking beasts and today's mobile devices have just accelerated our ability to consume and create content while doing other tasks, often moving other parts of our body. Despite my own beliefs, I am just as guilty of not practicing what I preach, of "moving and using." I also have a feeling that many of you are actually reading this now on your mobile device and moving in some way. Habits have formed and many of us have to wait, walk, talk, and drive while using our phones, despite the increasing news of accidents, laws, and prohibitions against it. When we are consuming content—rather than creating it—I have observed that many people use the device with only one hand and engage with the content using only their thumb.

Think about it. Watch your own habits and dexterity. Your thumb has become the most critical navigation finger when consuming content of all types. You swipe, press, touch, double tap, close, open, and share with the just the touch of the thumb. Sure your other fingers may come into play, but the thumb is criti-cal to mobile experiences and consuming content. *Consuming* content is very different than *creating* content, such as e-mails, texts, posts, and videos, and I want to draw this distinction.

Let's go back to walking while navigating mobile content. Believe it or not, walking requires at least one free arm swinging for balance. As long as one arm is free, you can use the other limb to easily navigate mobile content primarily using your thumb. If you don't believe me, trying walking in a safe, unobstructed area and use your phone with one hand. Now, watch yourself interacting with content where two hands are required. What do you tend to do? You stop. It's almost involuntary. Maybe stopping is actually a good thing, but it is contradictory to every reason why we use the phone to aid our ever-moving lives. Stopping is not in our vocabulary, or at least certainly not in mine. So if I have to employ two hands, it's probably more annoying than enjoyable, and in my experience, you are most likely to abandon what you're doing if you have to employ two hands to do it, especially if what you're doing is not critical to your next task or getting you from point A to point B. And, like it or not, most advertising messages and activations are not critical.

The example of walking and navigating mobile content defines, in my mind, where the stark divide exists in determining if you have a mobile-optimized experience. Many brands think they have a mobile-optimized experience, but if there is a pinch, squeeze, or pull involved where multiple fingers or two hands have to come into play to get the desired content into focus, that experience isn't ideal. It also means that there is probably too much content or features vying for visibility. Or you may have been sent to a non-optimized website where the destination you're looking for isn't clear or working properly. The more complications, the more likely you are going to either abandon the entire experience or not fully interact with the content and features as intended.

Mobile e-mail and instant text messages were among the first features created for smartphones, and the vertical scrolling mechanism was designed to allow easy movement and interaction with your mailbox. The phone was intended to be held in just one hand and the screen manipulated with your thumb. Don't overthink what makes mobile optimized. You have features and apps such as e-mail and contacts right on your phone that give you a great guide in terms of designing single-thumb functionality.

Assuming the content activated on the mobile device is related to an advertising source, designing for the thumb requires clean and simple navigation with larger type or visuals. Think about how clean and simple many apps are. They're easily visible and the content is easily navigable with your thumb. It's as much about marketing the experience and making it easy to navigate as it is trying to innovate some new type of functionality. After all, the best designs are the ones already used most on mobile devices for consuming content. All have employed a ladder design that makes navigation very easy with the swipe of a thumb.

GETTING TO OPTIMAL ON MOBILE DESIGN STARTS WITH A PENCIL AND PAPER

The first thing we need to explore is architecting an experience. Think about a marketing campaign you are currently working on or contemplating. Arm yourself with some of the earliest forms of communication technology—a pencil and single piece of paper—and trace the screen of your iPhone, Android, or other type of mobile phone. Now cut it out and begin to draw how you envision the brand experience, content, and navigation working. Use more than one piece of paper for each screen that would appear in the experience. Think of it as similar to a house's architecture or to a web's wireframe, the common term in tech speak. It's as simple as drawing basic boxes, circles, and handwritten text, but it allows you to visualize the experience with a screen the size of your own mobile device.

Before you take your architecture to design, spend a bit of time with your little paper cut-out, walking, pretending you're engaging, and considering if the experience is optimal both for use and in support of your marketing effort. If so, continue creating different cut-outs and sketches for different parts of the marketing plan, be it for TV, radio, print, or in-store interaction, because each platform may require a slightly different mobile experience and architecture to achieve the intended results. Often, we find that a brand may have four or five different ads running and each could require a slightly different architecture that would support it.

Next, I also consider the proximity of content menu buttons to each other—these are the buttons I will use to navigate. Think of this as the "mall directory" or "subway map" to the experience, the very first screen a consumer will see. Many brands jam pack the front screens of their mobile experiences or supposedly optimized web experiences, leading to users unintentionally pressing the wrong things and getting frustrated when they open the wrong feature. Load times are slowed by complex designs, and abandon rates naturally increase, especially for passive visitors, which most of us are when it comes to brand experiences. To visualize this, think about how many times you receive e-mails that end with something like, "Please excuse typos. I just have big thumbs tapping small letters." We have recognized the need to apologize in advance on every e-mail because consumers have come to accept the shortcomings of touch screens and/or their thumbs not hitting the spot their brains intended.

The content presented needs to have space to "breathe," to be visible at arm's length, and to have room for the user to touch. If the content is too small or overlaps in any way, you are back to difficult navigation in addition to the loss of a valued consumer. In many mobile experiences, I often see so many menu items that I have to manipulate the screen to the point of wasting time, an especially acute nuisance if I am only passively interested in the content. And, trust me, most times I am only passively interested in the content.

Here's another analogy. When PowerPoint was introduced to the business market, it created the most powerful and dangerous business tool at the same time. I became the "PowerPoint jockey" of my office back in the early days, but as the skill spread, so did the decline of the art of presenting. Suddenly 20, 30, 40, or more words began to appear on slides. People were expected to read what the presenter was saying. Presenters were using the slides as scripts due to laziness, lack of time, lack of understanding or some combination of all these reasons.

However, as training proliferated, the critical rule of thumb that stuck with me is no more than seven words should be on a slide. That's it—seven words on each PowerPoint slide. Many are shocked to hear this even though the tool has been around for decades, and they likely sat through a presentation recently that fully violated this rule of thumb. During my early career days, I would advise my much older mentors that if they needed more words to serve as the script, they should use the speaker notes. (It's amazing to me that many people still don't know that the speaker notes exist for this reason.) You can apply the same rule of thumb to mobile campaigns. Just because we can get more than seven words on the screen doesn't mean we should do it, and in fact, we should opt for less is more in every case.

Go back to the paper sketches. In my first drafts of sketching any mobile experience, I allow myself to get down every feature and word—even if initially in excess—to what I think will deliver against a campaign or brand initiative. I then start thinking in head-lines and become ruthless in how I can streamline the experience—limiting words, employing few graphics, or eliminating all the way down to just two or three base features that will support the objectives of a campaign. I know you have heard it a thousand times, but less is more, especially when you're dealing with a mobile screen not much bigger than a credit card. Even with the advent of Web 3.0, where web designs for computer screens automatically resize to mobile and portable devices, I still find the experience does not allow for easy navigation, access to features, or design. Apps, too, struggle with the proximity of content. Many still feel too crowded or make the mistake of trying to be all things to all people.

IS VERTICAL OR HORIZONTAL DESIGN BEST FOR MOBILE?

It's important to also consider how to navigate content from a functional perspective. However, I think it comes back to what people are used to with other phone functions, such as reviewing e-mail, engaging with Facebook, finding contacts, or looking at text messages, all of which offer scrolling features built for easy movement with the thumbs. When it comes to scrolling content on a mobile screen, vertical movement feels more natural than horizontal.

Just look at your contacts list or address book, wherein you see an alphabetized list of your contacts. You scroll up and down until you find the contact you want, and when you open the contact's information, it too is presented in a way that allows you to scroll through the information vertically. This is a very good way to present any marketing campaign screen because the user is already accustomed to vertical scrolling.

While we are all still experimenting with this as a mobile industry, horizontal navigation may work well with products in a catalog app or site, but vertical navigation still works best for photos, videos, text-based features, and other similar items. Why? I take my cues from the time-tested cable industry that still stacks channels up and down. They were the innovator of video content discovery and, in my opinion, they still have it right.

My business and life partner Mark Berryhill, who works with me on mobile projects and is one of the pioneers in branded video, comes from a TV production background and says, "Content—especially video content—still feels like it needs to be scrolled up and down. The consumer has long become accustomed to this navigation and changing it now is both counter to their nature and to their habits."

From a design perspective, I have also found that if you design a standard content framework to scroll from side to side, then you are greatly limiting the space you have for titles, icons, and social sharing, among other features. When you stack content titles, such as branded videos, vertically, you have the opportunity to add more content and features, as well as space for the individual to see clearly what you are presenting, and most importantly, to tap it. Side-to-side motion works extremely well for thumbnails of pictures, primarily for well-known logos of branded consumer products because you need no other descriptor. The minute you need to describe a feature that is not obvious—and increasingly, most content choices won't be—you need the space both for the eye and for the thumb.

Recently we were working with one consumer product brand on a major campaign, typically referred to in marketing and advertising circles as a major "tent-pole" event—a highly visible event such as the Olympics, the Christmas selling period, the Super Bowl, etc., that usually involves spending a large amount of sponsorship or advertisement money. The brand had created dozens of videos at significant expense for the event that were just waiting to be discovered on its website and YouTube page. The brand managers wanted all the views to be counted on YouTube. Our task was to construct a mobile hub that would be activated when the consumer was watching the brand's TV spots. Similar to music detection, we utilized Shazam to allow the consumers pick up the sound of the TV spot. With one tap of this app, the brand would send consumers to where they could watch the videos instantly on their mobile devices.

The goal was straightforward—get as many YouTube views as possible. But this is where the simplicity ended. The company's mobile web experience was very complex and would not work as a single solution to the mobile activation of the short campaign, which would only last a few weeks. The mobile site for the company was intended to support all marketing efforts and brands with features that endure longer than a campaign of such short duration. And, the site did not contain any of the videos that were housed on YouTube. We had to start from scratch and create a whole new mobile site, pulling in a few videos from YouTube, and selecting features from existing websites as well as other newly created content, such as product information and special pricing offers, that were unique to the marketing campaign.

I had a series of conference calls with the brand management as well as agency executives who were charged with the television spot creative to get their thoughts on the best way to create mobile activation of the videos. I asked for their ideas, but it quickly became apparent that the managers in charge of the project had never designed or built an experience for mobile video. Come to think of it, neither had I. Undaunted, I forged ahead, knowing that the creative process would benefit from more brains at work.

The creative team working on the project was brilliant at storytelling, but didn't understand the mobile distribution of the stories. In fact, they didn't understand why someone would engage with their TV spots to get more content on their mobile devices. When I walked them through how TV spots, print ads, and even out-of-home marketing could engage consumers further with their brands via their mobile phone, it was an epiphany for the entire team. One executive exclaimed, "This will change the face of marketing!" They were hooked and now began to lean in on the design and experience creation exercise.

Our attention turned to design and maximizing discoverability of these amazing videos. It was not easy. Not only were we dealing with a significant amount of content, but we also had to deliver it in a way a consumer would find appealing, could easily navigate, and would stay engaged with for as long as possible. Worse, the challenge from the CMO was to turn 30 seconds of advertising—which is where the consumer was prompted to take action—into several minutes of content viewing on mobile.

Together, the brand team, the ad agency, and I put the consumer front and center and began to create an experience that would appeal to the identified market. I began to look to the most obvious consumers in my life. I talked to my kids. I talked to my mom and dad. My partner Mark spent hours framing it with me. And Mark kept saying, "Don't overthink it." I took the content, boiled it down to two main navigation buttons with each one leading to a similar category listing relevant videos; these two buttons were all that would appear on the primary navigation page. The videos would flow in a vertical menu when you opened each button. We added stunning, eye-catching visuals, necessary headers, and minimal titles for each header and video. Then, the designer gave it room to breathe and be "thumb touched." On top of that, we achieved a first of pulling YouTube videos into the mobile with views still counting to the overall YouTube numbers.

We definitely achieved the goal of turning a 30-second TV spot into a mobile campaign where the consumers engaged for multiple minutes with the videos we presented. Our brand client was thrilled. But to be honest, what we did was so groundbreaking that I'm not even sure where to look for comparable metrics. We are just at the dawn of mobile activation of traditional media and it will take time to compare these results to other similar mobile results, which will yield consistent, relied-upon measures. Shazam and Nielsen, among others, have begun to put forward the start of industry measurements, but more will evolve as more and more traditional campaigns are mobile activated.

When designing for mobile, don't get lost in the technology. Go back to the basics. Think like a consumer. What do they want? How would they navigate it? If a campaign is appearing on TV as well as in-store point-of-sale (POS), for example, the mind-set of the consumer may vary greatly depending on how they interact with the campaign. You need to design for each type of consumer, considering their mind-set as well as the objectives of the campaign. If you keep the conversation grounded in the consumer, then the development, the case for investment, and, ultimately, convincing the consumer is far easier. Delivering the experience so they can navigate with just thumbs keeps the design and functionality clean, airy, minimal, and more visually engaging. Despite the fact that you can do so much more with today's mobile phones, the functionality thrives when it's simple and easy to navigate.

Never before have we seen the explosion of a technology that is now in the hands of nearly half the world's population. Marketers are beating their chests and increasing minuscule mobile marketing budgets, but in a few short years, I predict mobile will be front and center on most marketing and media plans—commanding as much attention, and possibly budget, as any other platform today. In fact, I would say that if even the most established brands in the most mature businesses don't figure out effective mobile marketing, they will be made obsolete in the tap of a thumb.

CHAPTER 1: THUMB'S UP TIPS

- Mentally take yourself out of your job and put yourself 100 percent in a consumer mind-set. Consider platform (tablet, laptop, smartphone) and location/activity (shopping, watching TV, reading a magazine). Now ask: What do I want from my brand on mobile?

- Test your mobile touchpoints—web, apps, social pages—on different mobile devices at a phone store. Do the experiences work on most phones? Do you like the experiences as a consumer? Does it support your current campaign?

- Your brand's mobile experience is truly mobile optimized if:
  - It works on a majority of mobile devices.
  - You can navigate a majority of features and content with just your thumb.
  - The content can be seen without excessive pinching or pulling or prodding it into focus with two hands.

- The mobile content for a brand's campaign should only contain two to three content features or menu items.

- Design for the thumbs and the eyes; keep the navigation clean, simple, and with larger type or visuals.

- Trace your phone and start to sketch the optimal mobile experience for an upcoming brand campaign for each facet—TV spots, print ads, in-store experiences, or on your website.

- Vertical navigation tends to work better than horizontal, especially if you need to add titles, pictures, or share features.

CHAPTER 2

Mobile Is the *Action* Screen

Stop Calling It "Second Screen"

THE TERM "SECOND SCREEN" HAS PROLIFERATED on the scene almost as quickly as "mobile optimization." Many of us refer to the mobile screen as part of the second-screen family (which also includes iPad, iPod Touch, DS Gameboy, etc.), because it is viewed as the companion screen to the "primary screens" of TV, magazines, web, and even in-store point-of-sale (POS) displays, among others.

Let me cut to the chase: I hate the term "second screen." In my humble opinion, the second-screen moniker was invented by people who toiled in traditional media and wanted to suppress rising technologies for fear of the financial impact to their revenues and bonuses. Unfortunately, the same trend appeared in the early days of Internet advertising. Plus, the term "second screen" immediately connotes that it is less important than the supposed "primary screen." From a consumer perspective, it could not be further from reality, as one could argue that mobile is the *only* screen used increasingly by younger and younger consumers. I look at my youngest child, who is still in grade school, and he is accessing a majority of his entertainment on second screens.

Carolyn Everson of Facebook concurs. "Second screen is a false notion. Our research shows that the average consumer checks his or her phone more than 100 times a day. For many of us, looking at your phone is becoming more and more akin to blinking."

THE CASE FOR THE TERM "ACTION SCREEN" FOR MOBILE

Rather than referring to the "second screen," we should introduce a new term: the "action screen." Mobile is primarily where brands and content providers *should* be giving the consumer the opportunity to take action, and as a result it is equal to or even more important than the primary screen. The fact is, all screens have to work in concert. However, mobile screens are where we can increasingly take direct action by bookmarking web pages and offers from brands and then watching branded videos and shopping later at our convenience.

The primary screen—still very much rooted in traditional media—is obviously critical and the one that largely initially alerts and builds awareness with consumers to what the brand is offering, as well as tells the consumer what the benefit is and how they can take action. While mobile can be a primary screen for advertisers, awareness building among consumers is still viewed as more efficient and effective over the primary screens—TV, print, radio, and computer screens, among others. As a result, I often refer to them as "alert screens," a designation—much like using "action screen" instead of "secondary screen"—that I propose we adopt instead of "primary." I still believe for the foreseeable future that "alert screens" will be quite vital in reaching a wide swath of target audiences quickly, efficiently, and effectively. Now, we have the opportunity to bring in the mobile screens or action screens where consumers can complete a purchase, engage with extended branded content, or bookmark product information for later when their program or reading is done or they have time to review before shopping.

Beyond engaging with the brands, mobile screens also allow the brands to engage with and get instant feedback from consumers. Never before have we seen the consumer's voice unlocked to such a level where they contribute content, ideas, opinions, buying intentions, and satisfaction levels to the overall brand experience. There's no more hiding for brands that don't perform well. With such an uninhibited two-way form of communication that our phones now provide, it's really not possible to keep referring to mobile as secondary. The "action screen" is now taking its rightful place in shouldering equal responsibility in the marketing mix as the "alert screens" do.

EQUALIZE *ACTION SCREENS* AND *ALERT SCREENS* IN MARKETING CAMPAIGNS

When we continue to refer to second screens as such, the psychological effect is that marketers and business owners are less inclined to give their campaigns the budget, development, execution, and priority they need. Furthermore, because of their lower priority, simple everyday occurrences like budget overruns in alert screen campaign productions can often negatively impact or eliminate the action screen campaign executions. Thus, campaigns can potentially move forward without a critical component—the mobile devices thus limiting the consumer's ability to immediately take action—the ultimate desire of any marketer.

Carolyn Everson also highlights that "2013 is the year that the digital screens—largely driven by mobile—will eclipse the TV screen for the most time spent with, about 5.25 hours on digital a day versus about 4.5 hours on TV. This is the first time one platform has moved ahead of another platform in 65 years, when TV did it to radio."

Despite this very recent trend, many in the media value chain can still make most of their money and profits from today's primary screens rather than the smaller action screens simply because you still can't beat the concentration of people watching the same show at the same time. Most creative ad agencies make most of their money from running copy and producing 30-second spots and print campaigns. Most of an agency's media buying arms still make most of their money from buying 30-second spots to execute campaigns. And brands live and die by how their CEOs feel about those 30-second spots and the subsequent budgets bestowed upon them for future campaigns. We know this is changing given the shift to mobile marketing budgets, but the limited focus to date on the rapidly emerging space tells me that brand marketing organizations and agencies have not fully realized or delivered yet on the importance of the action screens.

David Sable, CEO of Y&R (Young & Rubicam), the venerable 90-year-old advertising agency, says this about changing creative product: "People are hungry for great content. And mobile, with its wonderfully portable, ubiquitous presence, gives us real opportunities to take a 30-second spot and amplify it with extended content and brand engagement. In fact, so many experiences today begin or end with mobile, it's integral to anything and everything we do."

The action screen is the only screen that has the distinction of being with us from the moment we are first alerted to a brand offer on TV, to listening to a radio ad for the same brand as we drive to the store, to perusing the aisles and checking out of the grocery line. It's the action screen that can really aid a consumer both before and while they shop as well as build loyalty for and ease future purchases. It's the action screen that processes more data than ever before: it captures the initial action during an advertisement, the sites visited, and locations where brands are purchased. And it's that action screen that can be critical to managing the ongoing relationship with consumers, especially if they are under the age of 40.

Many in the industry who primarily toil in mobile also share this point of view. I recently read a white paper by Nellymoser—a big name in mobile activation—which indirectly validated the action screen term in its push to call QR codes "action codes." QR codes, or "quick response" codes as I originally referred to them, are often seen in print ads that appear as small, jumbled-up crossword puzzle–like images that you can scan with the camera feature of various apps to immediately take the action or visit the website the brand is offering right on your mobile phone. If we undertake the discipline to refer to second screens as action screens in everyday meetings and while budgeting, planning, creating, and executing, this subtle change in vernacular can have a positive impact, getting people to pay attention in meetings, lean a bit further forward with dynamic solutions, and embrace the real notion of what action we want consumers to take with a campaign. Then, senior staff can execute against it with the budgets and resources required. No longer will important screens sit or be referred to as secondary, and instantly we can advance marketing as quickly as the mobile phone advanced our lives.

Wendy Clark, SVP of marketing for Coca-Cola, concurs. Regardless of what we call the screen, mobile has to have a seat at the table. "In meetings and with campaigns, we have to be diligent that mobile is now a permanent part of every effort. Budgets need to be allocated and plans need to be executed."

I have to agree with Wendy. Mobile has to have a place in the media value chain each and every time. My goal is to create a shift in our vernacular to ensure that mobile's position in our plans, discussions, and executions happens sooner rather than later.

Recently, my partners and I worked with several brands that were creating experiences on Facebook, but functioned only on computer screens, omitting the action screens. The brands put their entire energy, budget, and resources into creating Facebook-functional apps, yet when I asked if it was possible to pull that same app or some of its features into a mobile experience, they responded that there was no budget approved to extend the experience for the mobile phone. This was their plan despite the fact that a recent study from Nielsen reported that more than 46 percent of people in 2012 accessed social media almost exclusively using a smartphone. So why was this sophisticated group of marketing and branding professionals hesitant to extend their app to the mobile experience? Part of it was timing; both social and mobile were such new phenomena that the budgets—approved 18 months prior to the campaign—were not sufficient for the development required on all platforms. The company executives vowed to change this for future campaigns based on the ability to now activate their spots with such technologies as Shazam and QR codes and the overwhelming evidence of mobile use.

No marketing book is complete without referencing the old Wanamaker's department store cliché: "I know half of my advertising money is working, I just don't know which half." With more than half of the population exclusively accessing social media with mobile phones and brands not investing in true mobile optimization of their Facebook and other action screen experiences, I can tell you which half is probably not working. Right now, brands are planning for the next three to five years and maybe longer. It is very likely that both mobile and tablets will surge well beyond current levels, and action screens must be factored into campaigns, budgets, and creative planning at far greater rates of investment that will ensure touching the increasingly mobile consumer.

Sue Kaufman, a veteran media buying executive with a long history at Group M and Y&R had this to say on explaining the value: "TV advertising is still the most intrusive—interrupting your experience and coming at you whether you want it or not. That's why it builds awareness and resonance. Mobile by nature is less intrusive. These kinds of activations are valuable because they are user initiated. I love the idea of alert screen for TV and action screens for mobile."

GOING FORWARD, ENSURE EVERY ADVERTISEMENT INCLUDES MOBILE ACTIVATION

If you have gotten this far in *All Thumbs*, you are probably fully on board with the importance of the mobile screen to your marketing efforts. However, the bigger your organization, the more likely you are to face ignorance, resistance, naysayers, or those who continue to snub the importance. So, how do you really integrate a mobile strategy into your overall plans three or four years out?

First, go beyond acknowledging the critical importance of action screens and make a resolution to set one simple goal for yourself and your organization. From this day forward, when creating a new marketing campaign, you will strive, encourage, and work to implement mobile activation from any alert screen that's part of the overall strategic effort. If I were a CEO or manager of a brand, I would ask with every campaign, "What's the action screen strategy?" While you may not be successful with every effort—even those you control and fund—the mere habit of asking each and every time will start getting everyone involved thinking about it, and will almost certainly lead to action, implementation, and, ultimately, success.

MARKETING CAMPAIGNS WITH ACTION SCREENS MUST BE MORE THAN A WEBSITE OR APP

While pushing for mobile experiences as part of marketing campaigns, we have to be cautious that campaign-driven, action screen experiences aren't a repeat of what has been created on a website or a company-wide mobile app. Oftentimes, the action screen is one where we have to create several different unique experiences for each marketing campaign with many being just a few weeks in duration and each possibly targeting different audiences. Then, we have to factor additional modifications to each mobile experience depending on the delivery over different platforms and different locations (e.g., home versus in-store versus TV).

It's really the responsibility of everyone involved in a marketing campaign to dissect the campaign and determine how the action screen can support each marketing campaign's objectives. This includes looking at where the alert screens will be touching the consumer, the different consumer segments, and the actions consumers will take depending on where they are. In my experience, a marketing campaign has much more specific objectives than can be satisfied by sending a consumer to a general web page or mobile application.

In some cases, a brand may want to extend its experience from 30 seconds of a TV spot to three or four minutes of viewing branded content on mobile screens pulling from YouTube. In other cases, brands may want consumers to bookmark new products or styles for when they shop after seeing a product on television. Or, brands may want to deliver useful how-to content in-store to aid consumers in understanding why they want to buy a product and maximize their experience with it.

Each part of the value chain and delivery mechanism of a campaign must be examined to ensure that the action screen experience directly leads to the action the brand wants the consumer to make. Many brands today still take users to a main web page on the mobile experience whether it achieves the campaign goals or not. If it is not directly related to the reason the consumer engaged with the brand on a mobile device, it will result in consumers not taking desired action, and the brand will fall short of campaign and mobile expectations. Such failed efforts lead to diminished enthusiasm and will be reflected in the ongoing budgets for including an action screen experience. It's a vicious cycle that can be improved if the entire experience from primary to action screen is fully contemplated, designed, and executed to support the objectives of a campaign.

In looking at what kind of action screen should be delivered, brand teams are required to ask such questions as, what are the actions we want different types of consumers to take at different times of their day during a single campaign? Then, what is the unique mobile architecture and designs of these individual actions? What is the experience like from each alert screen (print, TV, store window, or radio)? Is it the same or should it be slightly different for each one? What are the locations and times of day the campaign elements are being seen by consumers and what is their mind-set during these times? All are critical factors to ensure that the campaign hits the stride in marrying mobile experiences with overall campaign objectives. The great news is that the flexibility of mobile for geography, time, location, and, increasingly, platform, will allow us to tailor mobile action screen experiences.

An example of this is what we proposed for a toy manufacturer with heavy retail presence and significant ad spending budgets in the TV space. The mobile experience that starts with a TV advertisement could deliver a coupon to the mobile phone to encourage parents who may be passive or ambivalent about the brand to go to stores. Different from TV, the in-store experience for mobile could be one that gives product information; other incentives could include a free video or app download with every purchase or allow parents to alert other friends and relatives with a "gift request."

Regardless of all this recommended and obvious examination to build the optimal action screen experience, there is another common misstep often made where brands simply send a consumer to their mobile app or website and call it a day. I noticed this tendency in the early days of QR codes and I increasingly see it today with the activation of TV screens through apps such as Shazam. In many cases, marketers have to rely on (and were likely convinced by) a company's IT team that their mobile app or website, developed to satisfy company-wide goals, could be used for any campaign regardless of objectives. Unfortunately, this is not the case.

Sue Kaufman, an ad industry veteran with Y&R and Group M, says this: "There is a difference between a mobile optimization and a true effective mobile activation. An optimization simply makes your current site easily accessible on a mobile device (not an easy task). But a mobile activation actually takes into account the 'what.'"

I witnessed an example of mobile activation during my visit to the New York auto show where QR or action codes were on displays throughout the area of one luxury automaker and on all of their brands. I was really excited to see the action screen being employed to sell cars, and I thought, "Finally, the auto industry is leading the way." However, when I went to scan the code thinking I would get customized video and other content created just for perhaps the most important auto show in the world, I was met with a page from their non-optimized mobile site to help me find a local dealer. No sexy video of the car taking curves? No interior shots for me to share and look at later when I'm shopping for a car? No video on the fuel efficiency or safety performance of the car? I abandoned the page in an instant and thought my expectations were just too high.

I noticed other people scanning the codes. I cautiously approached several and asked about their experiences. They also thought it was flat and disappointing. One eager consumer wondered out loud how much they spent to build the displays around the cars, including the QR codes, how much was invested in developing the QR codes, and how much time it took to convince their bosses to do it, and yet the experience failed to do anything more than deliver a hard-to-see, faceless, nameless, and emotionless dealer page.

Think about it this way. Would you take a TV spot and run it over and over again from campaign to campaign, maybe altering the voiceover or on-screen graphics? Or, worse yet, would you run the same spot over and over again despite the fact that it did not strategically support your campaign objectives? The same principles hold true for the importance of the communications and messaging process of the action screen. You need to have the vigor, discipline, and insight to apply the same approach to every screen involved in the marketing mix from TV to live displays to mobile.

Going back for a moment to our auto example, let's pretend that the company actually did deliver a cool experience that got lots of social sharing and buzz. My experience at the auto show may be very different than if I am activating a 30-second spot pushing low-interest financing or a print ad in a very specific, targeted auto publication. Each and every time you ask consumers to take action with a different campaign or a different aspect of it, you need to think through what the unique experience will be on their action screens. Fortunately, we are reaching the point very quickly where we can decipher in a split second the different media through which consumers are ingesting our advertising, and even the types of devices they use, so we can deliver a unique, but intended experience with each one.

The mobile experience should not simply be a reload of the website. Sure, there may be portions of the website, branded content, or Facebook app that can be repeated in the campaign-specific action screen. However, the flow of the menu, presentation of these features, and mobile design will vary significantly. You don't want to be going to your digital people every time you have a new campaign—which sometimes can happen every few days—to change the mobile app or website to support it. Asking for that level of support is ludicrous, cost-prohibitive, and impossible to engineer from a time perspective. Have you ever met a group of tech developers who told you they can finish something before you need it?

In her vast experience, Sue Kaufman adds, "The problem is that we spend months and hundreds of thousands of dollars developing TV spots and websites and then need to use them forever. Action screens are different—think of actions more like promotions. Short term, relevant, action oriented."

Recently, I worked with a major liquor brand on producing recipe videos for its various products and then proposed activating a mobile experience in-store so consumers could download the videos right to their phones. The brand found that some of its consumers—especially around Christmas—were not exposed to its marketing, yet they were making critical buying decisions right in the store aisle. We proposed to the marketing team that they think about the critical buying decision criteria and create a mobile experience for in-store only, leveraging the graphic displays.

During the idea development process, we held a conference call with the brand's team to review our recommendations and designs, including accessing the recipe videos, positive consumer reviews about the brand's tastes, and additional holiday party ideas, leading to conversion of sales. They loved the ideas and asked if I could stay on the phone while they brought in their head of digital. He patiently listened to the entire presentation and recommended approach, asking the question that makes me cringe: "Why can't we just use our website that we spent the last seven months optimizing for mobile?" A very logical question, and potentially one good enough to put a halt to the entire project.

We applauded them for having a comprehensive website, but explained how the limited real estate of the mobile screen means you have to deliver the two to three actions relevant to the campaign or risk losing the consumer in trying to navigate the web experience. The in-store experience also only offered one feature: "Get Tasty Food and Drink Recipes for Your Holiday Party." The mobile experience should only offer these two primary features with recipes underneath a button for each: "Food Recipes" and "Drink Recipes." There was a third feature I suggested, which could take the user to the website if they wanted more information. However, rarely is a website going to support a campaign promise like food and drink recipes without altering the site completely every time you do a campaign. A website should be evergreen—providing a wide range of content, features, and information for a wide range of campaigns, products, and audiences. It's going to be one that you evolve with time, company objectives, and available budget and resources. Together, the web content supports the company, but the site's parts need to be tapped to deliver on a campaign—that's what we look to create in such mobile experiences. The head of digital quieted during our call as it was clear the marketers were inclined to go the suggested route of simply offering the recipes over mobile devices. It proved successful, and now the campaign is being readied for increasing sales, brand awareness, and engagement.

Seasonal campaigns, such as those used during a few weeks of a holiday period, are fleeting. You want campaign-driven mobile experiences to be limited in features, fluid in design, and even disposable at the end. You should certainly pull aspects of the website or mobile app into a campaign's action screen, but it should not exclusively dictate the experience, just as a company's digital team can't possibly change their "fixed" digital assets for every campaign. Similar to how we shop in a grocery store, we should pick and choose among existing web features before putting these selections into a custom mobile experience that is effective in supporting and delivering on the campaign objectives.

CREATING ACTION SCREENS FOR CAMPAIGNS THAT ARE EFFICIENT, EFFECTIVE, AND DISPOSABLE

We tend to construct mobile experiences for campaigns that are flexible, inexpensive, and ubiquitous to most devices. I join many in recommending building HTML mobile "houses" for campaigns that selectively pull features from the "fixed digital assets" of a company or brand, whether they exist as product information on the website, as app downloads or content on YouTube, among other existing features. These mobile houses mimic apps in functionality, are low cost, and can be "redecorated" very quickly from campaign to campaign. Oftentimes they're really just a compilation of features to meet a campaign's objectives, not an entire company's or digital department's objectives. In fact, in many cases you can leverage the video and other assets created for alert screens, such as 30-second spots and certain web features.

So let's take our liquor example where we created two buttons for food and drink recipes during the holidays. This same mobile experience can be repurposed for Valentine's Day for consumers looking to cook a romantic meal. The primary features don't have to change, and maybe some of the recipes don't either, but all you have to do is repopulate the campaign with content to what is seasonally appropriate, change the graphics, and you are off and running with the same experience you originally created for the holidays. It's very efficient and allows for much quicker updates, especially as the brand moves into the spring/summer entertaining season and subsequent holidays.

HTML, as a technology language, also allows for creating templates that can be re-populated from campaign to campaign and season to season. As a brand manager or business owner, you can focus on the experience knowing that with HTML, you can create almost any design and effect on the mobile device. HTML is a basic software language that, like many of the devices it operates on, is improving with time, becoming more widespread among developers around the world and cheaper to execute. In fact, it's far less expensive to develop than an app, as there are now many resources utilizing HTML to create a mobile web experience that is every bit as functional and fast. Every brand manager and business owner—large or small—can now create very effective and app-like experiences in HTML for as little as several hundred dollars. Building a mobile campaign experience in HTML is also a great way to tap existing features that a brand may have on its website and other virtual places and bring them together in a simple, easy-to-navigate experience. HTML coders can easily create these affordable and disposable or reusable experiences.

When we were working with a major candy bar maker to produce 30-second TV spots and print ads with a well-known celebrity, we asked the brand managers what additional content their consumers would like to receive from these ads through the action screen. We went through a range of ideas from fitness to lifestyle, how-tos, and food recipes. We were able to include this additional content in the production schedule and secured the important digital rights for the spots, saving a significant amount of time, money, and effort. At the same time, original content with the same thematic messages was produced for the action screen, and it would also live on the brand's website and social pages along with the celebrity's pages, extending the reach beyond what was originally planned. Overall, producing for all screens in mind simultaneously created savings and additional media value worth about $10 million, increased consumer engagement, and helped provide a 20 percent lift in sales.

To create the action screen experience, we decided to include three features: recipe videos to help people use the brand's products, a mobile coupon that could be scanned at checkout, and general product information. In each case, we found that the brand's website did not have all of these features. We tapped YouTube to house and host the recipe videos and created a mobile program guide similar to the one on your TV screen. The product information was already housed on the brand's website, so we simply linked to the mobile-optimized page. We had to create the scannable coupon for grocery stores from scratch. We then developed a front-page navigation in HTML housing all of these features, even though each one had a very different source. The brand saw a rise in awareness, time spent with videos, record coupon usage, and unique visitors to the website.

Creating and deploying the action screen requires many departments within a company and their agencies working in tandem. This is probably the most critical and difficult step to achieve. I began my career in the agency world when creative and media buying were all housed together. Fast forward several decades and with today's separation of such functions, I am still stymied, in many instances, that a brand's creative agency might have never met or worked closely with the media buyers. This division can often prevent the creation of an action screen, or more so, it increases the risk that any effort gets abandoned quickly.

With the action screen, we need to all work together to create the experience, execute media buys of the enabling technology such as Shazam or QR codes, and analyze the results together. There is little doubt in my mind that as mobile becomes increasingly important in the marketing mix among other reasons, we are going to see more and more brands begin to move the creative and media buying functions closer together or possibly, housed together again.

Recently, we worked with a major men's line of grooming products where there were probably a half-dozen agencies involved in creating and executing a campaign. The development of a companion action screen was largely driven by the media buying agency because they saw it as a way to drive the sampling of a new product that would be ordered through the mobile screen, thereby providing much-needed data about the individual consumer. The mobile experience created for the brand was built to achieve this objective and the CMO was very excited about the prospects.

Not everyone agreed on the introduction of a new way for consumers to get samples. Some of the creative team did not want to initiate a call to action onscreen because they thought it would detract from the 30-second TV spots, which were created at significant expense using A-List Hollywood talent. As a result, they did not want to ruin the spots with a small bottom-screen overlay that would drive viewers to the action screen. While they initially lost the battle, the creative agency eventually convinced a lower-level advertising manager to pull the call to action on the spots and eliminated any traffic to the mobile experience.

It was really disheartening to see this abandoned, especially after seven days of strong results across the spots where 10 percent of viewers continued to the mobile action screen, with more than half that number ordering the free sample and providing a wealth of data in the process. The CMO who wanted this mobile effort to begin with was on vacation and thus out of the loop, and the campaign ended before corrective action could be taken to retain the mobile call to action. As a result, we watched the thousands of viewers who took desired action in the initial days dwindle down to just a few dozen after the activation was pulled. All of us have experienced these sorts of internal disagreements, especially when a number of people are involved in the mix. Upon returning from vacation to find out the mobile activation was pulled, the CMO was furious as he was driving the use of mobile to activate. He called a meeting of all involved to postmortem the experience.

I attended the recap meeting some months later where the disappointing results were presented and the action screen experience was classified as the one failing point for the overall campaign. The creative agency then used it as a case to shift even more money to the alert screen or TV screen production, and they proposed leaving any mobile activation to them—thus revealing their true agenda. While it was not how you want an effort to go, the inclusion of the mobile activation screen really requires that everyone—from the creatives to the media planners and buyers—be involved in the development from the outset, and that they all agree to the objectives and use of the mobile screen and work together to achieve the desired result.

CHAPTER 2: THUMB'S UP TIPS

- Let's start the movement to refer to mobile screens as "action screens" instead of "second screens." In tandem, I propose referring to the "primary screens" of TV, magazines, and online as "alert screens."

- Place action screens on equal footing with alert screens for budgeting, planning, programming, creating, and executing. This subtle change in vernacular can start motivating your people to support overall marketing campaigns and make them far more effective.

- Set a goal from this day forward that ensures every campaign or social application is mobile activated from any alert screen—traditional to digital, in-store, and out of home.

- Resist the temptation to redirect all campaigns to a company's website or its mobile applications. Campaigns are fleeting, lasting just a few hours to a few weeks, and the related mobile experiences should be created to accomplish campaign goals, not just to tally redirects to a company's web page or mobile applications.

- Designing mobile campaign experiences with languages such as HTML5 gives them the best chance to be easily experienced on a majority of devices. These experiences are very cost and time effective to develop for any campaign.

- With the action screen, brand teams and agencies need to work together to ensure a seamless experience and analysis of results.

CHAPTER 3

Beginning a Mobile Strategy

OK READERS, THIS IS MY VENTING CHAPTER. This is where I piss off anyone who has a bachelor of science degree or an MBA or a Master's degree in anything—accountants, engineers, coders, product developers, etc. From my experiences, advertising and marketing is a blend of both science and art, which is ironic given that completely opposite parts of the brain are tapped for each. Given the explosion of technology, the advertising industry has largely been guided by the ability to track consumers and digital data, and as a result, science seems to win out over the art of creativity. However, many in advertising will agree that great creativity still breaks through the clutter regardless of how well science helps you target. No matter which side of the equation you fall on, we all need to come together around the consumer and become what I like to term "consumerists."

WHAT'S A CONSUMERIST?

I started to reference this concept in the first chapter, but now it's time to dive more deeply. "Consumerist" is a term that I increasingly use to describe someone in a company that naturally and genetically puts the consumer first in almost every regard and becomes the consumer's staunchest ally even if it means lower short-term profits, pain in the face of negative research findings, and adjustments to product development and in creating marketing experiences that are practical and functional. Consumerist or consumerism is a function that should be a formal role in businesses today. Everyone in a company thinks his or her job is to focus on the consumer. But walk down the hall and spring this question on your CFO: "Consumers or profits—which one pops to mind first?" Then, do it to your CIO: "IP or consumers—which one pops to mind first?" Try it with your CEO: "Executive pay or...?" You get the drift. The CMOs will tell you it's their job responsibility to worry about the consumer, but the average tenure of people in these positions in major companies is about 20 months.

I believe in the philosophy that the "consumer is always right." Many brand managers and owners will always claim the same, but when it comes down to the ruthless business of profits, customers and service to them rarely retains the primary position. Even the most successful brands cannot be all things to all consumers, but they can ensure long-term profits by becoming true allies of consumers or by behaving as true consumerists and exceeding expectations. True consumerists listen to the consumers. They keep an eye on what they want and deliver against even if the short-term gain is not recognized as something other than an intangible on a balance sheet. Think about your own favorite brands. Chances are they have gone over and above expectations. More so, you are probably spending more with that brand, driving the profits and loyalty they so desire with all consumers.

In business today, especially in the mobile world, we get caught up in the breathtaking advancement of technological capabilities and data analytics that pinpoint consumers so accurately we can deliver a message to them whether they want to receive it or not. I made a rather substantial investment—in both time and equity—in a business that was run by a group of consumerists who delivered brands to consumers by simply asking them to fill out a profile about their hobbies, interests, lifestyles, and upcoming purchase intentions. And in return for volunteering information, we would match them to brands of direct relevance to their lives with offers and information they desired. It was a simple, yet 100 percent consumer-centric proposition, but it initially failed because advertisers and their agencies embraced the efficiency of automated and programmatic media buying instead of spending the time and effort on creatively reaching the consumer on their own terms. It's far easier to allow an algorithm to target the consumer.

Despite the setback, I learned from the experience and it did not change one important fact. Consumers know what they want. You simply have to ask what that is and deliver it. The mobile device will only call attention to this fact and give marketers the ability to make it happen. There may come a time, as smart devices become ubiquitous, to introduce a personal advertising platform like the one I failed to create...the first time.

CONSUMER-CENTRIC MARKETERS WILL WIN ON MOBILE—THE MOST PERSONAL PLATFORM EVER

Our mobile phones have become personal accessories with options that give the owners a sense of style, function, identity, and more. This means you need to get pretty personal with your consumers. And there is a fine line between getting personal and being offensive. Regardless of how personal devices are getting, it is staggering to see the exact opposite result of what you would expect with more personalized individual selling, as marketing and advertising messages are increasingly unwanted. These messages are being delivered in much the same way as they evolved on the web—as mobile banner ads, but also as more intrusive, unsolicited e-mail messages as well as text messages. Sadly, I think it will get worse before it gets better.

One example of evolving yet still intrusive forms of advertising is from the newspaper industry, which is migrating to mobile delivery. The more advanced and successful companies, such as the *New York Times*, have implemented pay walls that draw in consumers. However, intrusive banners still appear on the bottom of the small mobile screen, or sometimes the screens are completely taken over by ads between the moment you click a headline and a few seconds later when the entire article is delivered. In tests I have undertaken, consumers do not find this form of advertising appealing at all. Much of the creative still seems like it was built for a larger screen with many ads simply reduced in size and difficult to see on mobile. Ads that take over an entire mobile screen are particularly annoying to consumers, especially if the reader is already paying for the content. What we need to do as an industry is really think through how to deliver advertising with the mobile content in a completely new way rather than just applying old ad models of the past digital era as well as experiences that were meant for different and/or larger screens.

Oftentimes consumers will tell us things the accountants, product developers, and even some marketers don't want to hear because it will cost profits, defy technical designs they spent months building, or take too many resources to implement. Ensuring a good consumer experience may have costs in the short term, but it will mean a more valuable, profitable, and rewarding win for both the consumer and brand. This sounds like common sense, but where do we begin?

TALKING TO THE CONSUMER ABOUT MOBILE WILL SURFACE THE TRUE CONSUMERISTS

You have heard this before and will certainly hear it again, but to win in mobile, you have to talk to the consumer. Sounds simple. Sounds obvious. However, it is shocking how many companies—large and small—do not bother to ever engage with the consumers in an objective way to gain more understanding of how they should be marketing on mobile. Mobile is a completely new platform with much territory yet to pioneer, regardless of how small the screen. It is a golden opportunity to gain competitive advantage and, perhaps more importantly, to leverage tried-and-true research to quickly accelerate the future success of mobile marketing.

While a partner and management consultant in a major firm for more than 20 years before I started my own company in 2010, I urged my firm to start doing focus groups with consumers on emerging forms of mobile and digital technology and gain their reactions to potential new forms of advertising and marketing. I knew then that the arcane form of digital advertising could not simply be applied to or slapped against mobile. We invited clients to observe the focus groups, and we sat behind mirrored walls together to watch the random 20 or so participants we had plucked from the street, paid $75, and fed dinner. The sessions were wildly successful, because unlike standard focus groups that test products, entertainment concepts, or advertising messages, we were reviewing the latest developments in digital and mobile technology as well as the new forms of advertising to which consumers would be receptive. The subjects also got into the act by jumping up to the whiteboards and sketching out their own ideas for desired advertising experiences, especially with the still-emerging smartphones.

Many of our media and advertising clients who were true consumerists loved the sessions because they were groundbreaking in trying to create new forms of advertising. Some of my consulting partners and client executives squirmed, however. This divide allowed me to begin to differentiate between those who were true consumerists and those who were not, even though we all worked in consumer-centric, media businesses. The nonconsumerists barely cared what the consumers said. It wasn't conscious; if you called them out on the rebuffing of the consumer feedback, they would have balked at the notion. But you could see their unease as the rawness of consumer testimony ran in the face of nice, neat profit models, taxonomies for websites they painstakingly crafted, and long-established advertising models that they all surely thought could migrate from computer to mobile screen. I termed these people the "profit scientists." While shunning the messiness of the consumer feedback, there was little doubt in my mind they would eagerly listen and contribute to discussions on profits. The "profit scientists" would also migrate to the food buffet often found at consumer focus groups and strike up conversations with just about anybody to avoid hearing the testimony on the other side of the mirror. I took note of these people with whom I—a consumer-focused, business rule–breaking anarchist—could never possibly work and be successful.

On the other hand, the executives who were true, in-born consumerists almost wanted to jump into the session *with* the consumers and would take page after page of notes based on the reactions they heard to different forms of mobile marketing. They hung on every word as consumers discussed their ideal mobile and advertising nirvana. The consumerists would throw out ideas to the others in the room in response to every major consumer revelation. They loved the mess consumers created by riffing on what they wanted versus what companies wanted them to want. The consumerists among the executives watching consumers talk about how to engage with them on mobile also went to whiteboards during our sessions. They began to sketch and design new mobile models that would be appealing and ultimately win consumer acceptance and thus more revenue for their companies. These consumerists got it, but they are not the norm in corporate America.

I was brought up in a business world that was guided by the philosophies of the American business schools. American business educational philosophy focuses on arcane principles rooted in industrial-age thinking, which is all about thwarting competition and driving profits above all else. However, this general philosophy tends to limit consumer experiences to ones that drive profit and stay within the confines of rules either established by the biggest competitors and/or the technologies we employ.

Limiting experiences and competition among limitless mobile technologies that are advancing every day is obviously an outmoded way of thinking. However, in this era of distributed, high-powered mobile computers and social networks, competition has been obliterated. When a well-known celebrity reaches tens of millions of social followers and can sway buying habits with the tap of the "Enter" Key, you better take notice if you are E!, Bravo, or *People*. This new era of mobile marketing and channels formed around individuals and social networks causes all of us to consider business models that actually welcome competitors, as well as to put energy into creating new channels to market and swim lanes of business. It's no longer the era of thwarting competition or putting every cent of profit before the desires and habits of consumers. We must move to a new model of partnership, collaboration, and creation of experience that evolves with the mobile era or we will quickly lose ground.

As you can probably now tell, I have always been the disruptive innovator sitting in the corner of the room, taking apart business models, asking the questions no one will ask on behalf of consumers, and breaking molds of past business practices to see if we can re-build them differently, profitably, and most importantly, for the consumer. Many I have worked with love this kind of unconventional thinking (and thus led me to name my first owned company Unconventional Partners). Some people try to sabotage me and my ideas by saying I'm unrealistic, too biased toward the consumer, and have no appreciation for "how things really work." But I have always hoped my approach would be appreciated for its fresh and disruptive thinking that will advance companies and their mobile strategies.

GETTING PERSONAL ON THE MOST PERSONAL MARKETING SCREEN EVER CREATED

Consumerists and the art of consumerism have never been more critical than they are now as we embark on the most important era of marketing—incorporating the mobile screen and capabilities. There is little doubt that we have to "think personal" with the most personal devices ever created. The good news is that unlike other technologies that came before it, we are all getting to know the mobile device as well as we would a part of our body. Never before did consumers understand the working nature of their tech devices more—how to navigate apps and do new things, such as getting thoughts down to 140 characters—than they do now with the little mobile device.

This is good. In fact, you have to first look at everything you are developing for mobile like a consumer before you think about it from your chosen profession, be it a marketer, technologist, or accountant. When you start thinking about how to apply mobile in your business, many of you will be inspired and start investing the time in creating experiences you want on Saturday morning at home, not those that are conceptualized on Wednesday afternoon in your offices. The creative muscle is not voluntary and ideas will come to you from your own constant use of mobile devices.

But you have to dive deeper, especially with a screen that is with you 24/7. Think about it. When I was in college over 25 years ago, people were alarmed at the amount of time the TV was on in the household. It was always about 12 hours a day or more. Sure, the figures on average viewing time are now lower, but not by much, hovering around eight or nine hours a day. These are hard statistics for me to fathom because I have never been that much of a TV watcher, even after I decided to specialize in advertising.

Fast-forward to the introduction of the mobile screen and its constant presence, including that third of the day, on average, spent watching television. Mobile then becomes the go-to device for a majority of social networking, communicating, shopping, and, despite the rhetoric from TV trade groups, video viewing.

You have to design the mobile experience with this in mind. Never has there been a more personal device and a more important time to monitor the habits of consumers. I can remember the day when people thought no one would use apps. Now, we have seen thousands upon thousands created and billions downloaded. I am reminded on a continual basis of just how much different phones create different habits and how quickly they can evolve and change from day to day. In mobile there are no set rules, and guidelines are continuously changing, causing companies with rigid structures and processes to have to think quickly, efficiently, and flexibly, especially when it comes to advertising campaigns with durations of as little as four weeks.

Rich Riley, CEO of Shazam, says, "We are working with the creative agencies which have historically treated mobile as a foreign object or afterthought to the TV or other advertising creative. They now realize that mobile is critical to the overall marketing mix and can take a viewer beyond a 30-second spot to engage them for several minutes on their mobile device. It now expands the time limitation that has long plagued the television advertiser."

HOW TO BUILD DISPOSABLE MOBILE MARKETING EXPERIENCES VERSUS PERMANENT ONES

As marketers, we are now entering a phase in which we can't just view one set of data from one set of activity when monitoring how consumers use their phones with advertising and marketing. Brands are all creating digital sites, apps, and mobile campaigns all at once; successes and failures happen at once as well, and multiple sets of different data must be monitored at the same time. Each effort has a very different construct from the others. This is why we have focused on and advocated developing disposable, mobile-based experiences in support of short-term advertising campaigns versus the more permanent, fixed assets of mobile-ready websites or apps.

While the actual financial costs of mobile site and app development has come down significantly as expertise and technology has become more widespread, it is amazing how much time and effort goes into building these assets for companies. It takes a large village of people to weigh in on the wireframes, features, global versus local control, and so on. And it makes sense as these fixed digital assets are critical to the entire strategy of the company, and increasingly will become the primary window into the brand for employees, consumers, investors, media, and recruits.

The downside of developing these fixed mobile assets is that they often have to appease a significant number of stakeholders, with only one of these voices being the consumer. In addition, the amount of development or quality control time can stretch on for months, or even years. As one CIO told me recently, "It's like I'm building a house and there is never a close date and the punch list just goes on and on and on. I am now starting to dream about the punch list! I often tell my stakeholders that the time to make changes or development window will be three to six months. No one is happy, especially my subconscious!"

We need instead to develop temporary mobile features to support shorter-term marketing and advertising campaigns that last as little as a few weeks or even one major day-long sponsorship event. As mentioned, these campaigns will likely have very different features than those of fixed web and mobile sites, but they should still be free to pull features from these sites.

Just as Twitter set the abbreviated 140-character pace, we need to bring the same editing acumen to the mobile campaign experience. While you can certainly have a fixed feature on temporary mobile campaigns that allows consumers to download your apps or get to your mobile site for much more information, the number of temporary features in support of a campaign needs to be greatly limited to the key objectives of the advertising campaign.

We recently worked with a major cosmetic brand that was using the mobile experience to support an awards show. Initially, we faced the same challenge we always do, with the client believing they could just pull in their mobile-optimized website to support the awards show sponsorship. However, when we examined the mobile site, we found about 25 features and pieces of content, such as videos, photos, and text. On top of it all, the experience was not optimized for mobile. Thus we began a design phase considering what the consumer would desire in terms of experience on their mobile device during the awards show and selected a few features that would best complement the TV-viewing experience.

We realized that the awards show viewers wanted information on the nominees above all else. While many of the consumers watching may know entertainment or music genres, they can't be expected to know every nominee. By showcasing the nominees in a way that supports the TV viewing in a very simple, easy-to-thumb-navigate format, viewers would able to come back throughout the show, increasing impressions of the sponsoring brand and other related content.

Then, we suggested helping viewers get the fashions and styles they were seeing on screen. We suggested a second feature related to the nominees that would describe the trends in fashion, hair, and make-up, which were important to the advertiser. In pre-recorded video vignettes that featured the company's spokespeople and products, we delivered companion clips of no more than two minutes in length that complemented the TV viewing and that related to the most desired content on the nominees.

These two features plus a link to the brand's more fulsome website and mobile app were all that we provided. In reality, it's all the viewers could handle, and at the end of the day it's all they really wanted. Yet, they kept coming back to the brand's experience throughout the awards. The marketers were concerned at first because their inclination is to inundate the consumer with all the features they can offer instead of focusing on what the viewers wanted from this one awards show experience and brand sponsorship. It was a huge success, with one-third of the viewing audience engaging with the mobile campaign and two-thirds of these folks coming back three times or more during the awards show with multiple video plays and exposure for their brands.

MOBILE IS ALL ABOUT THE NEW
"KPL"—KEY PERFORMANCE LEARNINGS

One of the most critical obstacles in creating mobile campaign experiences are the ever-critical Key Performance Indicators (KPIs). For those who may not be aware, KPIs are commonplace in corporate business today as a way to measure success of almost any business initiative. They have especially proliferated from the top consulting shops. We are now obsessed with KPIs and often use them as tools to manage our people and truly understand success as well as weapons of "office politics" to destroy anything new. On the one hand, KPIs are a time-tested and successful way to run a business. On the other hand, it can be a devastating way to manage the development of such a medium as mobile that is just starting to emerge from its infancy.

In most instances, we have never seen the kind of influence that mobile has on our lives. As such, we have to introduce measures that allow testing to flourish along with the mobile experiences we create. As we are in the early days of building for this platform, I ask that executives and business owners consider employing the term Key Performance Learnings (KPLs). It's a slight tweak on KPIs, but does not have the same hard line of success/failure. Similar to KPIs, KPLs still hold everyone to some level of measure, but feature a strong layer of learning versus determining if a new use of a new platform was a success or failure. Learnings over time can evolve into KPIs.

Recently I was in a meeting with a client who had a person whose sole job function was to manage KPIs for every advertising campaign. As we embarked on the mobile plan to support a TV campaign, she started to apply old media measures to mobile. Clearly, this matrix measurement cannot work with a new medium. After much discussion, we agreed to call the performance of the mobile experience "learnings." Rather than setting up the program for failure, we initiated it to provide a set of results that would allow us to modify for the future campaigns as well as to work our way to mobile KPIs in the distant future.

Wendy Clark, SVP of marketing for Coca-Cola, agrees that as an industry we need to develop a unique set of measures. "At Coca-Cola, everything we do gets measured. However, for mobile, I like the notion of starting with a new set of learnings that are created for mobile and applied to future mobile campaigns, so that we can develop a unique set of indicators."

Learnings and the art of talking to the consumer will never be more important in the mobile age. As one who touches and guides many brands, my advice is to stay close to the consumer, listen to the kind of personal experience they expect, and deliver it with the most personal devices known on earth. Don't overthink the solution. Keep it simple. Keep it manageable. Make it disposable. And make everyone in your organization think and behave like a consumerist—train them, streamline agenda items to fit the philosophy, and, most importantly, learn from failures and successes.

Sue Kaufman, director of channel planning at Y&R, says, "It's like any new technology (and in the scheme of media, mobile is still new). Consumers use it in ways we can't anticipate when the techies are creating it. We need to watch what happens in the real world and be prepared to learn, adapt, and exploit. Quickly."

CHAPTER 3: THUMB'S UP TIPS

- Investment in focus groups and consumer testing is critical in guiding development of mobile experiences.

- When it comes to mobile and until we have repeated uses, we should introduce Key Performance Learnings instead of relying on Key Performance Indicators.

- Many brands are buying big tent-pole events such as sporting championships, awards shows, and sponsoring an entire season of a TV show, among others. In these cases, think of your mobile experience as though you were handed a program for a live show, and then visualize how you would integrate your brand into it. Consumers will come back over and over again.

- Make everyone in your organization think and behave like a consumerist—train them, streamline agenda items to fit the philosophy, and learn from failures and successes.

CHAPTER 4

When Your Past Mobile Marketing Efforts Have Failed

Don't Give Up!

MOBILE IS NOT A PASSING PHASE—FAILURE IN EARLY DAYS WILL BE COMMONPLACE

Throughout the last few years, I have seen seemingly smart executives who respond to a new idea or way to leverage a technology with, "Thanks, but we tried a mobile technology like that once and it failed." Failure is an option. Giving up is not, especially in mobile.

After all, Thomas Edison reportedly failed at the light bulb several thousand times until he finally got it right. Steve Jobs and Steve Wozniak failed so many times getting to a first-version, wood-encased Apple 1 circuit board that each reportedly sold his most prized possession—a VW car and high-end calculator, respectively—in a last-ditch effort to fund one final attempt. It was ultimately a success. It took Alexander Graham Bell more than two years to develop the telephone, and when he finally hit success, he could only utter in disbelief: "Mr. Watson, come here; I need you." Imagine if all of these guys gave up on their first try or after a few failures.

OK, so let's stop the life-coaching lesson. The reality is that as waves of innovation take place, especially in the mobile space, brands are going to have to look for new ways to market, and before they hit on a success, they'll have to make many attempts and fail many times. Those who say they would not attempt again something similar technologically to a failed mobile approach is an obvious sign that this person is either too ignorant or inexperienced to believe technology improves over time or is trying to quickly diffuse the conversation due to laziness or shrewdness—to attempt the idea again when time has passed and people have moved on.

I was in a meeting with an executive at a major media company during the days when WiFi was quickly spreading throughout the globe. These were really the early days of smartphones, before we knew they were actually "smart" or could tell whether they would penetrate the market with any real scale—although analysts were predicting huge leaps in market growth in a very short amount of time. We were talking to this executive about several ideas to take advantage of the fact that people no longer needed to be wired to the web to interact with it. My business at the meeting was to present new forms of advertising for the media company to adopt, which would now be enabled by technology in the hands of consumers.

The executive said, "We keep hearing about consumers taking mobile computing with them on airplanes, listening to music while they tap out e-mails, and shopping online while they download coupons—I just don't get it. We tried some things like this before and it just didn't work." He said this in 2007, just a few months after Apple released the first iPhone. You may wonder about that executive: He's no longer with his company.

With new technologies, we have to realize that they're going to evolve while we sleep. This happens with every wave of innovation. With billions of people on the planet, innovation is constantly happening, and in pockets of the world we would never expect. But new technology advancements, especially in mobile, take time— you can't just expect it to happen on the first go. You must also be patient when setting expectations for what a consumer will do with new technology. In fact, you should always leave room for how a consumer will behave with it or what the experience that you build on it will look like. As new technology is released to the marketplace, you have to react to it by applying your understanding of consumers to the experience and be prepared to adjust . . . quickly.

So how do we move ahead to cultivate the best experience possible when working with a new technology, especially one like mobile?

KEY STEPS TO SETTING A COURSE FOR MOBILE MARKETING SUCCESS

We have to remember that we will fail multiple times while attempting to leverage any emerging technology for a new form of marketing. If we're stuck on setting metrics based on either past performance of proven experiences or company objectives, we will fail and likely not try again. There is nothing wrong with setting expected metrics—but using the terminology introduced in chapter 3, "learnings," will help us manage expectations, soften shortfalls, and broadcast that we are here to learn and hopefully succeed, but likely not all at the same time.

Wendy Clark of Coca-Cola believes we "need to stop comparing mobile results to other forms of media and start comparing them to other efforts on the same platform. The more we do, the more we learn. The more we learn, the better we can measure. And regardless of the platform, everything at Coca-Cola must be measured. It's just how we do it that must advance."

Corporate politics, jealousy, and a need to stay ahead are other reasons failures can be magnified. However, even if you have the most benevolent of cultures, you'll receive different perspectives from person to person and from different participating departments within a company on any new form of marketing. In other words, each person or department may not cooperate in the way that makes a test work in the intended way. Using "learnings" as opposed to metrics in your language goes a long way toward keeping the "corporate bullies" at bay as well. It also helps manage executive and board-level expectations. And it gives everyone a chance to ask "What did we learn?" in the aftermath instead of playing the blame game.

Next, you need to cultivate new technologies, such as mobile, and not try to overextend in execution, resources, and costs. Product and marketing teams are the worst abusers of their own innovations, in my experience, as they will often try to put too much into them. Just because you can do something with a technology doesn't automatically mean you should do it. You have to really focus on what is going to be initially essential and then what you can add incrementally to a consumer experience, especially in the mobile world. New features and functionality are still evolving, along with consumer behavior. Rushing too much ahead of the consumer will rush us to failure.

DON'T LET MOBILE MARKETING
TESTS SPIRAL OUT OF CONTROL

It's easy to let a simple test spiral out of control into something much bigger and unintended—ideas sometimes never get to execution because the scoping spirals out of control. One example of this occurred when we were asked to propose on a new mobile experience to test a campaign created for a cosmetics company around one of many red carpet awards events and leveraging the brand's sponsorship. Beauty-based consumer product companies love red carpet events. The idea was to provide the viewer of the red carpet event with mobile content from the brand, such as how to get certain make-up looks or forecasting some of the hottest colors of the season as seen on the celebrities. I was asked to work with the "digital" agency, which admittedly had little experience in mobile activation, and given a budget for a $75,000 "test," which, if confined to the parameters and budget, would have succeeded.

However, the proposed effort quickly blossomed into a $3 million attempt to set the entire company's digital, Facebook app, and mobile strategy for the next year. The digital agency saw a huge revenue opportunity and the mobile test quickly got subsumed in the effort.

Even if the initial test had produced multiple results, it quickly got ahead of itself and became an out-of-control attempt to add many moving parts and resources. The company was trying to innovate where no one had ever before to stretch the technology to places the consumer would never go on their own with the brand. The effort's visibility to many in the company and their subsequent involvement consumed the effort. Even, the CEO, CIO, and CMO would appear intermittently on our daily project management calls to check progress, ask budget questions, and make recommendations based on whims they had in the shower that morning, completely changing the direction in the blink of an eye at 8:30 on a Wednesday morning, and again the next Tuesday, and again the following Friday.

Because of the size and sexiness of the project, the top executives had briefed the board on their mobile prowess and, in essence, sought the budget approval. We were doomed. What had started as a small test on mobile with a big, high-profile event quickly became a "Trojan horse" for both management and the agency to overhaul the company's entire digital strategy. There was no way we could expand the focus of the original plan in a logical or timely manner, especially to take advantage of the upcoming sponsorship. Slowly, the consumer experience was overtaken by product, technology, and marketing departments—all with competing interests and expectations. Soon, the consumers got left by the wayside, and you could even see the development and marketing teams beginning to plot blame before execution failure even occurred.

The original test on mobile of showing women how to apply their make-up and get ideas for updating their colors to match the season was no longer the focus. The much larger agenda and budget that would impact most every digital aspect of the company created a political mess and would take months if not years to sort out. They were no longer working toward a success or even a test launch of mobile—which was for an event just weeks away—as originally intended. They were working to start managing a failure of the much bigger agenda all saw coming, or even to politically capitalize on it.

The original idea for the sponsorship and a small test budget came and went. The opportunity to have at least a partial success was now a distant plan and memory. The original $75,000 investment to move the innovation "ball" a few yards down the red carpet of consumer experience fizzled, and the rest were scared to ever try anything like it again.

TECHNOLOGY OF ALL TYPES TAKES TIME TO BECOME FLAWLESS

Technology is always emerging and takes a long time to work its way to flawless performance. However, many of us who are not technologists often approach a technology with unrealistic expectations of reliability. My dad often cautions when I am looking for a new car not to buy one in its first model year because it will take a while for the "glitches" to work their way from consumer to mechanic to production lines. The same is true for mobile.

Just because a mobile computing technology is able to do something, we must be cautious that we don't expect it to do it all out of the gate. Initial tests should be confined to tight parameters and to the teams undertaking them. Campaign-specific tests should be confined to campaigns. Broader-scale projects that are company-wide, such as mobile optimizing a website or fixing a Facebook application, should be set aside as separate initiatives.

While I will cover this later, I once worked with a magazine group who were just blown away by the ability to unlock more information from print media on a mobile device through then-new QR codes. The first attempt to introduce QR codes to the consumer experience resulted in a hodgepodge of features that really had no purpose or draw. As we progressed, we realized that the activation had to be purpose driven and related to the content for the reader to engage. While this may sound obvious, it's very easy to get caught up in attempting to do everything that's possible versus what is simply expected by the consumer.

Initially, I didn't admonish them or dissuade them from attempting to add more features, such as giving the reader opportunities to write the editor, share a recipe via e-mail, or enter a contest by submitting the best picture of a dish they prepared. I loved all the ideas and knew we could add those in time. But we needed to limit the first attempt to one or two features, such as the ability to download a recipe or stream a how-to-make video. From there we could test consumer reaction and expand as needed. Unfortunately, some influential people involved in development wanted to add multiple features, and they succeeded in trying it this way. The ship to failure had launched. The consumer failed to engage. On the next go-round, we all agreed to temper our desires and focus on just one or two purpose-driven features that matched the content, and we saw increased success. While initially this success was defined as a just a few hundred interactions among several million readers, we knew this would only grow.

In addition to being overly ambitious on consumer features, the technology was still emerging (and indeed still is) to support all that we desired. When we attempted this campaign with some of the original features, many consumers did not have smartphones yet, and their devices were overwhelmed by too much content. Features failed to load quickly because of limited bandwidth and current functionality of the devices. We expected too much of the technology, and the consumers did not engage. Aside from the fact that we had too many features, the technology was still not fully reliable. We arrived at technological failure.

The immediate blame was placed fully on the technology. In part, the blame should have been placed on the people managing the technology and test instead of the technology itself. We also should have scaled back the consumer experience. Despite all of my preaching on the subject, I can still get stuck in a vortex where I expect and plan too much and attempt to overfill the consumer experience. In this age of mobile, a good rule of thumb for initial campaigns is definitely less is more.

DARE TO DREAM YET BE
PREPARED TO SCALE BACK

The key to success in your approach to a mobile campaign is to start the consumer experience with a blank slate. At the beginning, go crazy. Dream. Scribble across paper and whiteboards with unbridled imagination. As long as you can do it technologically, write it down. This is your chance to think big without being encumbered by budgets, execution resources, or any inhibitor to achieving success.

Once you have a grand plan, start to scale back. Be ruthless in the process. Pick one, two, or at most three features to attempt. Remember, you have to support the marketing objectives and the campaign has to be digestible within the budget, timelines, and technology limitations. Set up the entire mobile experience for success and growth. Even if you have scaled back an idea or feature, keep it in mind to fold into future iterations. It's better to have incremental success than massive failure. Hopefully this will help fortify you with confidence, fill you with ideas, and help you manage your own mobile pioneering for maximum learning and success.

CHAPTER 4: THUMB'S UP TIPS

- Commit your company to advance its marketing in mobile. Don't deviate.

- Don't allow a mindset of failure to thwart new tests and experiments. In mobile marketing, ban the statement, "We tried that once and it just didn't work. . . ."

- The reality is that as waves of innovation take place, especially in the mobile space, brands are going to have to look for new ways to market and will fail many times before hitting on a success.

- Embrace failure! Failure in innovation should not be a negative thing but a learning experience.

- In mobile, focus on the entire consumer experience. The technology is often blamed when the culprit is actually the consumer experience.

- Take a "learning" approach for new mobile marketing tests. There's been nothing like mobile, so comparing it fully to traditional media measures is unfair to all, especially consumers.

- At the beginning, think big. Then be prepared to scale back to one, two, or a very few features.

CHAPTER 5

TV and Mobile

Skip Skipping, Cause Pausing

IT'S AMAZING THAT FOR ALL THE ADVANCEMENTS in technology, the two most precious commodities still remain: time with a brand and attention to it. Dating back to my time as an advertising major at Florida State, I remember the professors pounding into us that our ads must not only reach the most desired demographics, but they also have to be creative enough to break through the clutter and not be missed or switched off. This is not new, and it's still echoed today, from the halls of Madison Avenue to the awards stage in Cannes that annually recognizes the world's most creative advertisements. The conventional wisdom is that good creative will get watched, great creative will get repeat views, and amazing creative will get shared, by word of mouth and now social networks.

WELCOME TO THE AD-SKIPPING GENERATION

Fast-forward to today where not only do we have the technology at our thumbs to fast-forward through TV and display ads on mobile, but we also are all becoming proficient at knowing exactly how to time and speed through TV ad pods with the effectiveness of a video gamer. As a consumer, I both love and hate this phenomenon.

During my last Christmas shopping excursion, I realized that I was completely out of touch with the latest trends. From an advertising perspective, I was asleep. I had so perfected skipping through TV spots—I never saw a single ad—and with the power of satellite radio, I paid to skip ads in my music choices. As for my online subscriptions, I upgraded my subscriptions to certain publications to ad-free levels, and I have mastered ignoring every ad from Yahoo! to Facebook. As I type, I can't recall an ad that I've seen on any of my most commonly visited digital content providers.

As a consumer, I wasn't just skipping out, I was missing out. How could I be this out of touch with new trends and products? Sure, ad skipping may have made my entertainment time more efficient, but it killed my consumerism. Being out of touch was disturbing, especially because I rely on my living from advertising and the consumer.

MOBILE CAN HELP CREATE "TWO-WAY TV" AND TARGET THOSE READY TO BUY

Many of you still believe that there's no advertising like TV and traditional advertising to build awareness. Many consumer brand managers still tell me that when they advertise on TV, sales go up. Many of you reading this also make a pretty good living from traditional advertising. But even still, brands always yearn for more engagement, more data, and just more interaction with TV spots. As Rich Riley, CEO of Shazam, says, "Regardless of the success of TV, we identify the brand with our audio detection technology, and in doing so make TV spots 'clickable.' They get this and they want this."

Several leading marketers that I have worked with over the years have told me the same thing, that there is waste in TV media buying. Even though the desired target audience of a given TV show may largely be within the same age bracket, gender, and life stage, not all of them could possibly be the consumers most likely to buy. We all know that there is waste in any media buy, but the question is, how do we isolate and engage the consumer most likely to buy? The interaction mobile devices provide could suddenly start to make waste in TV media less important, especially when you are able to involve those who will engage with your brand and possibly buy your products.

Mobile allows us to parse a target audience to those most likely to buy. If you ask a marketer how many people in a TV audience of 5 million will actually buy the intended product, the answer may be several hundred thousand, at best. Introducing mobile activation to this audience can increase the identification of the most likely buyers significantly just by allowing viewers an easier way to take action, bookmark items for shopping later, and/or sharing information with friends, thereby increasing purchases. Of course, we have seen the integration of URLs, Twitter handles, and Facebook pages into 30-second spots, but rarely have I seen a URL that was short enough to recall, yet up on the screen long enough to really cause meaningful action. However, it does give me hope that the advertisers will embrace the integration of mobile on the screen.

Getting viewers to interact with video on TV has been the Holy Grail since I began in the media industry. Working with AT&T on new forms of advertising across multiple platforms, I had the pleasure to be one of the first Americans to experience IPTV (internet protocol television) or U-verse®, the brand name many recognize. I actually like to call it "two-way TV" because the high-speed nature allows individual viewers to engage with the content and save it for later, tag brands and "file" special offers, or share with friends instantly on Facebook and Twitter. When you are watching a 30-second spot, the IPTV technology can allow the user to go to the product website right on their TV screen. It really is ushering the next wave of "smart TVs" that allow you to surf the web, buy products, and communicate with friends all with your remote and TV screen.

By moving away from such tech terms as IPTV or "smart TVs" to something like two-way TV, we start to condition consumers that they can interact and engage directly with the content and advertising.

Rich Riley describes the results of making TV spots interactive: "By applying our technology to TV spots, we have in a sense made them 'clickable' and have seen engagement rates of up to 10 percent of the entire audience. This is 100 times the success rate of standard digital ads, and we can track the activities of consumers including interacting with a brand's content, downloading of a featured song, or making a purchase."

LET'S FOCUS OUR ENERGY ON
PAUSING, NOT SKIPPING

I don't understand why distributors—who rely as much on advertising placements for revenue and certainly profit—have not been dissuaded from making ad skipping so feasible. I mean, my car is able to go 140 mph, but I never drive at that speed. While the ad-skipping technology is readily available, the advertisers are working hard to figure out how to get people to stop skipping. In fact, there is intense research, including my own, on the subject, using focus groups that took place when the skipping technology was first introduced.

I found in my research that a majority of people routinely skip ads and make no bones about it. There are times when they won't skip, but this is usually when they are distracted—they've turned their attention to an e-mail, the Internet, or a text on their mobile or other devices. Prior to ad skipping, we had become acutely aware of what we can do with the time provided during an ad pod, such as letting the dog out, going to the bathroom, getting a bite to eat, or retrieving laundry to fold. So in some ways, ad skipping has actually been going on for years. It's not a new thing. What I did find in my research is something that could be an interesting trend to carry forward in the mobile activation age.

During focus groups, trailers for major motion pictures tended to be the least skipped or the most paused-on form of advertising. Why? They tend to be the most creative advertising because they contain highly produced movie content. Thus, this bolsters the claim that good creative always captures attention. However, the movie industry employed a little advertising trick that came long before ad skipping, and it certainly helps slow it down for trailers. The theatrical creative often employs opening billboards of two to five seconds telling the viewer what they are about to see: "Coming this Friday," "Now Playing in Theaters Everywhere," or "The Sequel to the Smash Hit Comedy," among other enticements to pause and watch.

This prompts the entertainment-hungry viewer to stop and watch what could be a good option for the coming weekend. The subjects who we tested thought this kind of "billboarding" was a great idea and wondered why other types of advertisers didn't employ the same technique. One woman in our research said, "Look, I may not watch every ad, but I'm constantly on the search for new products, samples, coupons, and incentives to buy. If I knew the advertiser was offering something like this right up front, I would likely pause on their ads."

If we carry this philosophy forward to the mobile age, we may see the opportunity to get those in a target audience most likely to buy to engage with their mobile phones. There are a plethora of technologies from Shazam to Get Glue, Zeebox, and others that allow the audio or app-based interaction with 30-second spots and TV content. By considering applying these technologies—calls to action at the bottom of the screen and billboards at the beginning—to encourage slowing or pausing an ad that would normally be skipped, we may just tap a consumer most likely to take action and buy.

Shazam has expanded its music detection technology to TV, allowing consumers to engage with TV spots and content via the audio. Just like trying to find out the name of a band playing a song, Shazam works with TV content audio in just a few seconds to deliver the consumer companion content to whatever show or ad they are watching. All the consumer has to do is tap the Shazam app on their phone when they are prompted to enjoy the additional experience.

Shazam, one of the most downloaded apps in the world, with hundreds of millions of users and readily available on most phones, is a prime example of how brands can extend their experience from 30 seconds to several minutes with instant mobile access to branded video and other content, digital coupon offers or other savings, how-tos, and recipe ideas that can be bookmarked, and new products to share. In just a few seconds, a viewer is notified on a spot to take action and tap their mobile device for a whole host of activations through URLs, Facebook pages, and Twitter hashtags.

Up to now, advertisers on TV and radio have largely adopted using only URLs or toll-free phone numbers to drive engagement. During a recent Super Bowl, I counted how many characters were used in special web addresses to drive consumers to engage with the brand. I counted an average of 17 characters per single URL, and I thought this was too big a burden on the consumer to retain and then punch in during a 30-second spot.

Even with the promise of such technologies as Shazam that can pick up audio in a second or two and deliver a brand experience in just one tap, adoption of such innovations is still growing.

I find it confusing to personally see reactions of some resistance from an advertising industry that somehow thinks long URLs plastered across the bottom of TV screens for two seconds or web addresses in a magazine at nine-point type will somehow get magically processed, recalled, and typed into a an address bar. So, why is there such resistance to applications like Shazam that are seemingly vast improvements over current activations?

OVERCOMING THE CREATIVE HURDLES
OF MOBILE INTEGRATION

Some executives in the creative advertising community don't want to mar their clients' beautiful productions with a Shazam or another call to action onscreen. Yet, a majority of these ads still have some sort of visible call to action. These executives are following the well-trod path of skepticism in the early days of any ad tech advancement that we've seen throughout our discussions of mobile. Similar to when the web first appeared, we had to get used to delivering campaign-specific URLs. This took a while to take hold. Then we saw the advancement of Twitter and Facebook—along with the advertising community's initial negative reaction to sending consumers anywhere other than their brand's own website. Soon, brands got as creative with their hashtag callouts as we did with the headlines and copy they employed. It's now time to evolve again, and this time it's exploring how to activate TV and other creative with what a majority of TV viewers have in the opposing hand from their remote— their mobile phone. Mobile activation of advertising creative is no longer optional. We can improve the creative integration of mobile, and we need to start doing it right now with TV spots and other advertising.

Further, we are back to the same argument that even if you have a successful hand-off from an ad campaign to a mobile device, we have to work equally hard to be sure the experience on the mobile screen is of the same quality as on the TV screen. This, too, will take time to evolve. Many brands are sending you to their company websites or Facebook and Twitter pages with every advertisement, yet many of these experiences are not mobile optimized or are mostly unrelated to the campaign.

To help develop the TV campaign–specific mobile experience, many brands I deal with also have a plethora of existing content to tap, including how-tos, recipes, new products, content extended from sponsorships, media integrations, and much more. Much of this content will just sit on the media partner's website or YouTube waiting to be discovered, searched, or prompted by the marketing of the brand. Of course, many brands will spend significant sums driving views of their own content when they have not yet fully leveraged their existing media buys to drive activation. Unlocking this content from 30-second spots with mobile phones is an obvious place to start.

MEDIA BUYERS HAVE TO WORK WITH CREATIVES (AGAIN) FOR TV ACTIVATION

Many agencies—on both the creative and media buying sides of the business—are also negotiating bonuses on top of payment terms with their clients for generating a greater amount of awareness, activation, and sales. Increasingly, a number of brands and a few agencies have said that we must use mobile to activate the TV content to turn 30 seconds into several minutes of viewing of branded content or some other desired action that will lead to a sale, and we need it all to occur on trackable platforms. Media-buying agencies in particular are big on getting to a specific number of video views for their brand clients. While the media buyers are historically the biggest resisters of anything that upends traditional content, they are increasingly facing the pressure to get more out of every media buy. Mobile activation is great way to do this.

We worked with a vitamin-infused healthy beverage brand that created a significant amount of music video content specifically for a major sports sponsorship with a worldwide audience. The content was placed on YouTube, but it wasn't getting enough views to satisfy the brand's executives or provide a return on the significant production investment. My company was brought in to create a mobile campaign to drive people to the YouTube content on their mobile phones as well as to ensure that it counted toward their total number of views on YouTube. No problem, we thought—but then we started to build.

We began to construct something that, in our estimation, had never been done before—a branded mobile experience containing a brand's YouTube videos that could be activated with any mobile device and only includes the brand's videos from YouTube. The brand mobile activated their TV ads with Shazam to allow viewers to retrieve music videos on their phone. We were successful in constructing an experience that pulled videos from YouTube seamlessly and delivered them right to the viewer's mobile device, and views counted toward the overall number. From our understanding, this was the first time that such a mobile experience had been constructed. The entire branded mobile experience was working perfectly across a multitude of mobile devices. The brand converted a significant number of mobile viewers from their 30-second spots with an average of eight minutes of viewing time and experienced more than a third of these folks returning multiple times. Another mobile frontier had been conquered, and we proved that a brand does not have to search very far to find content to support a campaign or satisfy TV-spot mobile activation.

The best news is that we learned that viewers are eager to mobile activate content from TV commercials and their favorite TV shows. The question is, how can we start to get the right viewers—and I mean the ones most likely to buy within a massive target audience—to pause, engage, and enjoy additional content on their mobile devices? The challenge is not to buck the trends and the outcomes but to work as an industry to evolve creative, technical, and data standards to make the alert screens of TV the natural feeder to the activation screens of mobile.

Pausing on TV spots should become the mantra of the advertising industry. We need to stop worrying about ad skipping and the ever-evolving technologies that allow consumers to do it. We need to focus and develop creative that will alert consumers to take the desired action. Status quo is not the standard in technology, nor should it be with mobile marketing if we are going to keep pace.

CHAPTER 5: THUMB'S UP TIPS

- Don't focus on skipping. Give people a reason to pause and engage with your advertising.

- While your brand will still benefit from the broad awareness delivered by television, you can introduce mobile activation to your traditional TV buys to help target consumers most likely to buy and to take immediate actions that can increase the likelihood of sales.

- If you currently engage consumers with Facebook pages and URLs on your TV spots, then you are ready to engage with mobile.

- Research, select, and implement mobile activation technologies for TV, including Shazam and others.

- Employ creative calls to action in the form of three- to five-second billboards at the front of ads or text across the bottom of the screen that stays static during ad skipping. This will call attention to what a consumer can activate with their phone—coupons, samples, special offers, etc.—regardless of whether they skip through ads or not.

- Consider both the creative rendering of the call to action as well as the mobile optimized experience, ensuring that it is campaign specific.

- Resist the temptation to just send viewers to a company or brand website or a generic Facebook or Twitter page. Be sure the mobile experience supports the objectives of the specific campaign activated.

CHAPTER 6

The New Two-Fisted TV Viewer

Remote in One Hand, Mobile in the Other

AS I TYPE THIS, I'M WATCHING THE LOCAL NEWS on TV where they're covering a major weather event happening in my area. Suddenly, the anchor jumps up on the screen and tells the viewers to grab their phone and snap a picture of the weather in their area. I find myself obeying and dutifully taking pictures out the window, only to spend the next 15 minutes figuring out where to send them because the anchor failed to tell me. Now, I realize that I'm no longer paying attention to the newscast or the anchor, and I've even lost interest in the photography I was encouraged to do. I began to think that if the local television station had better integration with the viewers' action screens, I would have never taken my attention off the alert screen, and the network would have delivered a seamless, much more fulfilling experience. It highlighted for me the need to focus on the producer community.

TV PRODUCERS NEED TO EMBRACE THE MOBILE FUTURE

Action screens and, for that matter, user-generated social media, scare today's TV screen producers and programmers. Just like the VCR, DVR, and online viewing shook up the TV industry for years before it started to adopt measures and metrics, so too will it take time to integrate the action screen with TV viewing. Right now I fear that the best solutions we come up with are actually competing with TV content and advertising, creating even more resistance among TV producers and advertisers to participate. Yet the reality is that a majority of the 70 percent of viewers with smartphones (and probably nearly all of the 30 percent or more of you with tablets) are doing something on those screens at some point while watching TV.

In these early days of TV integration with mobile screens, we are seeing producers and programmers still trying to commandeer the experience by periodically popping up viewers' Twitter or Facebook posts and attempting to weave them into the programming. One can only assume that TV producers are hoping to encourage two-way communication with their audience by using a third-party social network. Yet the dramatic banter from the TV anchor and the accompanying on-screen graphics of "select" social posts makes it appear as though it's a huge social audience that's engaged with the show. I will often check out the actual number of people engaged either on Facebook or Twitter, and it's usually a very low number relative to the total TV viewership. Additionally, social interaction with TV shows that are not live can have a limiting effect on the audience and work against the goal of actual engagement.

Social and mobile screens have snuck up on us so quickly that networks have either failed to learn how integrate them with the TV screens or they have not added the appropriate producers for just these experiences. So, like advertisers, TV producers give action screen integration lip service before placing it second or third in the pecking order. If we really thought about the companion action screens, many shows have the opportunity to develop and quickly edit additional content that can be pushed through the mobile phone.

So, what are some basic examples of integration that complements TV viewing without competing with it? Sue Kaufman, an ad agency executive with Y&R, highlights some early successes that can draw in brands and viewers. "Jon Stewart, at the end of *The Daily Show*, asks the person he is interviewing if they can stay around and then directs people to see the extended interview on the web. Or, a great ad example is Bravo's *Top Chef* putting an additional competition on their website, accessible by mobile, and later integrating that competition into the main show. 'Last Chance Kitchen' was sold as a separate online and mobile sponsorship."

Imagine watching a major entertainment awards show like the Grammys or Sunday Night Football—while you have intense interest in the event as a viewer, you really don't know much about the nominees on the stage or the players on the field without researching them. Why not offer, with the tap of a mobile button, a fully optimized "one-stop-shopping" research experience for this type of information? And, furthermore, make the mobile experience sponsored to maximize all screens facing the consumer?

This is what I call situational marketing, which I think will be increasingly applied to mobile. Put yourself in the situation of the viewer and ask what kind of content they would like to have to go along with the TV content. This is really more art than science and best orchestrated by the TV producers. It's sort of like trying to figure out what appetizers would complement an entrée. As stated in our previous example, if you are able to easily access more information or details about award-show nominees or athletes so that you can better enjoy their performances, you may even be willing to pay to download songs, movies, or past games, or at least follow your newfound celebrity favorites and shows/networks on Twitter or Facebook.

Still, many of you will say, "I can just search on the show or participants to get that information." Sure, you can do this, but it is markedly more efficient and effective if producers and advertisers work together to tailor and enrich the experience. Furthermore, all of the possible content around a single show tends not to sit in one place online—the social features, apps, videos, and other experiences are spread among other platforms. Building a disposable, web-based mobile experience to support a given show, or even a single episode, allows TV producers the opportunity to connect the disparate parts, weave in brands, and direct viewers to a single destination with multiple features that maximizes the viewing experience.

David Sable, CEO of Y&R, says this about finding the balance: "TVs aren't going away, just look at how much of Twitter is all about TV. One hasn't replaced the other; in fact, they arguably make each other better. People still like the communal experience of watching a show together with friends and family. But chances are they are all sitting with their phones or tablets and hugely receptive to complementary content."

Recently, we architected and built a mobile companion experience for one of the sponsors of the Olympics. The brand team had created a series of several-minutes-long biographical, fast-paced videos of each athlete they were sponsoring, which were placed on YouTube just waiting to be discovered. The sponsor decided to engage with Shazam and add a call to action to each of their spots running during the Olympics. The content was presented in a very easy-to-navigate design in which all you needed— you guessed it—was your thumb. The average viewer went from a 30-second spot to spending several minutes with the branded mobile videos on the athletes—the extended time and interaction with the brand was viewed as a huge success. Many of the people came back multiple times, returns that seemed to peak with the events in which the sponsored athletes participated. Of course, the social shares among viewers were significant, as were the positive comments about the sponsor's efforts to support U.S. athletes.

Despite this good example of complementing the TV viewing by successfully incorporating content and a sponsoring brand, we still hear detractions from the creative TV production community for incorporating mobile action screens with their content. They see it taking attention away from the primary alert screens of TV, print, and other traditional media. But it is to traditional media's detriment to not understand how to incorporate the rising mobile experience. It's only going to accelerate, and opting out is not an alternative. Just take a look at some facts.

Apple announced that half of all apps ever downloaded were done in 2012 alone (that's 20 billion of 40 billion). These numbers are surely to be eclipsed. A recent study of 185 million smartphone users in India (keeping pace with United States) showed a 65 percent increase month over month in combined use of TV and mobile data usage with highest usage while watching TV between 10 PM and 11 PM, telling us that users are mobile surfing while watching. Shouldn't TV producers and advertisers seek to control this experience with such trending growth?

Rich Riley of Shazam highlighted a recent country music awards program where it reminded the nearly 10 million viewers prior to the show that they could Shazam during it. Shazam's data showed that there were hundreds of thousands of engagements with its app, and Riley concluded of the exercise: "We were now able to identify the users by device, what type of music and content engaged them, and deliver highly targeted messages. It was a win for everyone—artists, show producers, record labels, and of course, the advertisers."

PROGRAMMING THE MOBILE SCREEN WITH EQUAL FOCUS TO THE TV SCREEN

Assuming we have a mobile-optimized experience, we need to start programming the mobile experience with the same vigor as devoted to the primary TV screens. If we keep it simple, resources will cost far less than the potential revenue generated from new forms of brand sponsorships and inventory over the mobile device. TV networks and station executives alike tell me that their "digital" sales people are just sitting around waiting for something more to sell. I suggest mobile activation as the best opportunity for new, higher-value inventory than we have seen in years.

However, we have to create experiences that complement the TV viewing, not take away from it. If we take the leap and complement the viewing experience, we will draw in viewers as well as advertisers.

Let's go back to our example of big tent-pole events that draw a lot of advertising dollars. We definitely want to provide viewers with more information on performers, nominees, or athletes—creating a kind of a program guide to the viewing experience—and then deliver the experience as if viewers were members of the live audience. Then, we start to design the mobile experience that would complement the TV viewing experience.

When it comes to highlighting the performers or listings of celebrity participants, you'll need brief videos and social/share features on each participant. If there is respective content to buy—such as music, movies, or merchandise—figure out how to capitalize on impulse buys. Many TV producers I've met with have said they have hours of footage from backstage or behind the scenes that can be edited down to just a few minutes to complement the producer-chosen scenes we see on TV. Calls to action from on-screen talent and graphics should detail briefly what the consumer will get on their mobile devices, and call-outs should continue throughout the show. Extensions can be built in, allowing consumers to participate, contribute, and of course, share with their comments. We see pockets of this happening, but consistency will deliver the promise of reach and frequency that has never changed in the world of marketing.

In my opinion, to date Fox is the leading American network in including mobile activation with their TV programming. Whether it's allowing viewers to vote via mobile on *X-Factor* or offering a free download of a song during *Glee*, Fox seems to understand that the mobile experience must give consumers something of value. While this has started perhaps obviously with music-based programming, I think we can see this type of experience start to flow into sports programming as well as scripted television shows.

TV PRODUCERS HAVE THE ABILITY TO TAP UNAIRED CONTENT AND CREATE NEW AD REVENUE

Local and national TV news producers also have access to significant content that can't be shown on air, but can be delivered through mobile screens. This would allow the extension of viewing and brand experiences beyond what they were able to fit in the allotted time for television. If news programs or TV shows simply offered the entirety of interviews that they could only air partially as extra content for viewers to download, those networks would see a proliferation of off-hour viewing, especially with the power of Twitter and Facebook to pinpoint audiences of highest interest. They could also tease upcoming segments and prompt viewers to interact socially and stay connected to both the TV and mobile.

Beyond simply bringing to life a program-like experience to complement the viewing, we have to think about what else will add to the viewing experience that we can deliver over mobile. Like some of our fellow marketers in the consumer brand space, we, as TV producers and brand managers, need to ensure that the experience evolves from episode to episode. This may require additional resources, but the ability to involve advertisers should help pay for the cost of such experiences.

How can you involve advertisers? First, the mobile experience should be a *sold* experience with the usual banners and designs incorporating the brand's look and voice, and it should house special content and offers from the brand. Increasingly, more and more TV shows are selling full integrations as well producing additional content for the advertisers to use on their own web, social, and mobile experiences.

The mobile experience that's activated by TV show content can help tap the same audience an advertiser is seeking to reach, increasing touchpoints, impressions, and most importantly, driving activations. In my experience, if the content on the mobile/tablet complements the TV viewing, then all the brands involved get positive kudos from the viewers. Plus, with the new inventory, many TV producers can help their sales teams create new valuable inventory and revenue, becoming the virtuous financial cycle all TV business managers love.

Recently, we worked with a men's grooming company and women's cosmetics company on two major TV sponsorships—a major fashion-based show with celebrities and a pro sports event. In the fashion-focused case, the brand sponsored the mobile experience that operated very similarly as a live program guide, providing viewers with in-depth information on the performers, fashions, music, behind-the-scenes interviews, and preparations. In the other experience, the brand added video content, some of which was directly related to the program along with other pieces of content that were not, including one segment that was more than ten minutes long about the city hosting the sporting event, which detracted from the sports event on the TV screen and was not really relevant. Not surprisingly, the content not related to the sports event on TV received much less viewership than the content related to the talent and clothes appearing during the fashion event.

Additionally, the one piece of video content that was more than ten minutes in length had very high abandon rates after just a minute or two of viewing, as it likely detracted from the TV program. This may not be surprising, but the brand could have increased viewership of these additional pieces by encouraging viewers to bookmark the content and view it at a later time. Either way, I applaud the brand for trying different types of content, and hopefully the learnings will continue to aid in improving future mobile experiences in complementing TV viewing.

On the local level, we have worked with several TV station groups that used mobile activation to promote their free app to track weather, traffic, and local events, as well as to deliver bonus content on news subjects that could not be covered in the time they had to air. In both cases, the stations created significantly more inventory for their sales teams at higher advertising rates.

They were sold out of all available advertising inventory in just a few weeks on all platforms for the entire year.

So, given the growth of mobile and the significant revenue opportunities, TV producers will need to start putting mobile experience on equal footing with their primary screens. Similar to advertisers, this will take significant focus, discipline, and creativity. However, the rewards in terms of greater viewer engagement and revenue will lead to a greater investment in resources and experiences for all to benefit.

CHAPTER 6: THUMB'S UP TIPS

- TV producers and programmers need to start considering the action screen (mobile) as equally important to the alert screen (TV) when it comes to programming and producing.

- Think about your TV viewing experience as though you are seeing a live event. What would be in your program for such an event and can you replicate it on the mobile phone?

- Building inexpensive web-based and easily changeable mobile and portable experiences allows producers to effortlessly change the mobile experience from episode to episode, as well as to simply weave in advertisers.

- Seek ways to give major sponsors a presence in the mobile extension and further expand the opportunities for their target audience to take action.

- Start weaving in brands as added value to a larger TV buy or sponsorship, and then slowly migrate the experience to a premium or paid position. If you build it, they will come.

- Calls to action from on-screen talent (and continued call-outs during the show) should detail briefly what consumers will get on their mobile devices.

- Experiment with different types of content to see what will draw in viewers and shares on social networks.

CHAPTER 7

Read, Snap, and Enjoy

Mobile Just Might Save Print

NOW OR NEVER—INVEST IN
MOBILE OR GET LEFT BEHIND

It has been my goal over the last seven years or so to drive more value out of magazine and newspaper print publishing. Even today, I work with a number of celebrity and lifestyle magazines, and I can assure you that images and stories in print sell publications to legions of fans—even with huge social (and virtual) followings. Regardless of how mobile advances the transition of print publications like *Vanity Fair* and *InStyle* to electronic platforms, consumers still love to see fashions, their favorite performers, and other content in images with the richness and representation that only print can provide. Yet I don't need to overstate the research to show that if we include video with print pictures and make it easy to activate with mobile, a good percentage of the readership will also become viewership. If new forms of mobile-activated media are rising up all around us, why haven't the print publishers responded?

While there are pockets of hope in the print business, I randomly picked up a few magazines and newspapers from the best-known companies in the world. Few, if any of them, have meaningful connection to their digital properties or online videos. Why? Because most of these organizations still keep their digital businesses separate and, in fact, still struggle to sell features other than print. Many also still view the print product as the end game instead of a means to the end by fully leveraging the print product. Despite this somewhat negative assessment, many print titles still have huge assets, including their readership along with the data that comes with them. Yet, most publishers are struggling to maximize return on these assets by bridging them from the print product (and I mean every page of the print product) to a compelling mobile experience unique to the print product. Instead, we see the separate digital and mobile product teams trying to do everything on their own. Some succeed. Most fail. Yet, many, especially in the newspaper industry, are left wondering how they abdicated local "touch" to other brands, namely bloggers. Sure, many have made the tablet investments, but few have done the same with mobile activation of print to the degree needed, even as mobile device penetration has skyrocketed and still outpaces other screens.

IMAGE CODES, ONCE SHUNNED, NOW LEAD
THE WAY TO MOBILE ACTIVATION OF PRINT

But with so much promise in mobile-activated print pages, why have so many publishers struggled with the technology despite the fact that the glorious technology has been around us for years? QR codes and related print-to-mobile activation technologies are the most misunderstood and misused technology. For some reason, these little codes either meet with two sets of reactions—ardent belief in the codes, especially among many advertisers, because they have found that if used purposefully, the consumers will engage, or nonbelief in the codes, especially among many who produce the print products carrying these very advertisers. Some nonbelievers may even say, "We tried that once at our (insert print company) and it didn't work," almost as though they are saying, "We'll never venture into the print-to-mobile-activation world again." With the world going increasingly mobile, how can anyone possibly say this or stop attempting to find ways to activate print?

Despite the resistance among certain factions in media, I see QR codes everywhere—mainly used by brands rather than publishers. QR codes are literally overtaking most other forms of technology to activate print. And, you can see why. Who wants to type in a 19-character URL when the snap of a code will do the same thing in fewer steps or even one step? As I first discovered these little codes for myself back in 2007, I knew they would be the first step of many to bring print to life and provide a beacon for a slowly dying industry. As time has gone on, scanning apps have improved significantly, and a whole new virtual world can be opened with a single click.

A well-known example of a consumer brand using QR codes in its magazine print advertising is Procter & Gamble. It has incorporated scan codes and other technologies in print ads to allow readers to access video and additional content right on their phones. Our company has a partnership with American Media and the company's *OK!* magazine, with whom we currently produce a daily entertainment show. In the weekly editorial page of the print magazine, we provide a scan code for recurring features that allow readers to watch videos on their phones. While initial scans have been modest, we know that repetition will create habit and habit will create ever-increasing engagement. It's always about reach and frequency, regardless of the platform.

Beyond traditional magazines and newspapers, you can find scan codes everywhere. I just found a code shaped like a strawberry on my produce packaging that prompted me to find out how this little magic fruit fights cancer. There's one on my pasta package offering recipes and how-to-make videos. And I even saw another one in *People* magazine for Fruit Roll-Ups. There's yet another one on the health insurance premium bill from my provider that would allow me to access their mobile site and make the payment instantly. For all those people in the last few years who said they don't get QR codes, have "tried" them and won't try them again, or don't think they work, I sure see a lot of them everywhere. Maybe this is a marketing "Trojan horse" strategy? Deny with your words, but plow ahead with your actions, hoping only the consumer takes notice.

In writing this book, I wanted to see if QR codes are being used effectively, and I've sampled them all, from grocery packaging to the latest in P&G print ads. The activation is easy enough, and in fact recognition is improving everyday with apps that offer universal scan code readers. However, the mobile experiences vary widely among the brands.

Among those doing it well is McDonald's, which began to add the QR codes on the outside of its bags. When you scan the code with your mobile while eating your Big Mac, the experience brings to life McDonald's' sponsorship with the NFL, showcases its value menu, features special discounts, and more. Now, McDonald's could also leverage this same mobile experience by extending the scan codes to print magazine ads, newspaper inserts, and out-of-home marketing, among other platforms.

Citizen Watch Company is another leader in mobile efforts. The legendary watch manufacturer now employs these codes in its magazine ads to feature its state-of-the-art technologies. The experience is a rich blend of video, images, and compelling short-form text that redefines my opinion of Citizen as being on the leading edge in technology and design—both critical factors in my own watch purchases over the years.

Despite these good examples, I have found many others that deliver nonexistent experiences or have broken links. I can't imagine scanning a QR code on an ad or package and having it come up as, "Sorry, no web page found!" Yet, this experience has happened a number of times for me in my quest to try every code I came across.

Even if the code took me to a brand destination, many times the content was not mobile optimized, or it was out of date, or not related to the call to action. Sure, you can point your finger at technology as the culprit, but I would give the Fortune 500 a collective D+ for mobile experiences when activating print with the phone. The magazine and newspaper community would not even get a passing grade on its current mobile activation applications for its editorial content. As print readership and print pages shrink, so will the opportunity to convert subscribers to data emit-ting, readers, viewers, and loyalists. So, for those who want to fault the QR code or any activation technology, I say you are shooting the proverbial messenger, not the one who created the message.

Here's what I would do if I were a print publisher. I would add mobile activation at the end of every piece of printed content, including stories, articles, photos, recipes, how-to advice, etc. When activated it would unlock a host of content, including full articles, longer-form videos, shopping lists, buy-now or buy-later options, calendar reminders, and more. Activation can be done with scan codes or the emerging forms of technology, such as augmented reality being developed by Hewlett-Packard (HP) under the brand name Aurasma. In the case of Aurasma, your phone activates the camera feature within a publisher's own app whereby the reader centers the phone over a page to activate the mobile experience. Think QR code, but without the physical print code.

David Sable, global CEO of Y&R and one of the industry's top visionaries, says it best: "Every time a new medium is invented, there are those who predict the demise of everything that came before. In truth, the new media help us redefine the old and, together, they form powerful user experiences. Mobile, with its interactive, integrated, individualized capabilities, helps us create a seamless path between the digital and physical world. That is supremely relevant, because while digital, not everything is digital."

Programming your brand's mobile pages will be the most critical thing you do in the coming years as part of your market-ing and revenue efforts. Learning how to do it takes time, dis-cipline, process, resources, and, most importantly, content. To understand how we solve this print-to-mobile conundrum, it's best to go back to the history of such enabling technology and work our way forward to today. And, for those QR code naysayers, you won't be surprised to see that I take you to "ground zero" of this technological advancement.

In 2007, I was in Tokyo for an assignment. While there, I happened upon what was then a new technology: 2D bar codes or Quick Read (QR) codes, which proliferated throughout consumer tech stores in Tokyo. To activate them, people simply activated their camera feature through an app and held the camera lens of the phone over the codes, which looked like thumbnail-sized square boxes resembling jumbled-up crossword puzzles. Once I saw them and played with the experiences in the tech stores, I began to notice them throughout the city on point-of-sales displays, billboards, and even menus. Of course, each mobile experience was basic, but very brand related (or at least from what I could tell). My love for the burgeoning mobile era was enhanced on that very day.

QR codes were everywhere in Japan. Yet, each one contained a completely different URL that could be changed instantly, from campaign to campaign, season to season, and product to product. I quickly learned to snap a picture of the code, and with the tap of a finger I was whisked to an experience the brand thought its consumers would enjoy.

The first place I saw the codes was in a consumer electronics store filled with phones from a number of Japanese manufacturers. The codes were on the point-of-sale displays, and the shoppers who scanned them were able to access high-value production experiences with videos of products, pricing comparisons, and special offers. I stood there startled, but among a sea of consumers who were eagerly and effortlessly moving from displayed device to displayed device scanning the codes.

"Wow! This would revolutionize marketing with mobile devices," I thought. Out-of-home displays—which is where I mainly saw the codes—would be forever invaluable. But I also thought about the value this could drive for traditional TV, radio, magazine, and print newspaper, which could all be watermarked and activated for mobile. Everyone back home in the United States would see the radical possibilities.

One night, I went to a hot Tokyo karaoke club. It was a very young crowd. Most patrons were in their late teens or early twenties. I noticed that a lot of them had their own QR code tattooed permanently on their arms. Remember, they could change where the code took the scanner anytime they wished, so the code would never have to change. These tattoos were obvious permanent, personal watermarks. One second, the destination could be your Facebook page. The next minute, it could be your company's website. The next minute it could be a news article seconds after the person's favorite sports team won a match. Or, for nights like this, it could go to the Japanese equivalent of match.com to get personal data. The possibilities were endless.

Culturally, it was mind-blowing to see Japanese youth weave together a new form of personal activation that gave social details, exact location, and current desires into one experience. This is how content companies and advertisers need to construct mobile experiences. I was truly in love with what I thought would be the game changer for traditional to digital platforms with mobile as the bridge. I was just about seven years too early.

Sue Kaufman is an ad industry veteran who has represented such brands as Campbell's. She says this about the codes: "I suspect that skeptics (especially those who buy mass media) may point to the relatively low usage rate for QR codes. But that, I think, misses the point. The point is that you are enabling consumers who want more info to get it. And people expect to be able to interact with us everywhere, even in a static medium like print. If the codes don't get much usage, that's not the fault of the technology—either you have a relatively low-interest product (not everyone will want to interact with their paper towel) or your creative proposition isn't very compelling. Either way, don't blame the code."

MY FIRST FAILED ATTEMPT TO GET THE INDUSTRY TO ACTIVATE PRINT

Fast-forward to Fall 2009. I was the keynote speaker at a conference on innovation presented by the Magazine Publishers Association. I thought I would bring down the house with my Japanese discovery, and so did the head of the MPA. I felt that this was one of those turning points where I would introduce the concept of mobile activation of print magazines with QR codes (or really any enabler). Some of the more advanced attendees had seen the technology and nodded approvingly and ferociously as I spoke. But most others looked at me with that wonky near-yawn expression.

As I began my demonstration with an actual print magazine, I looked around at the blank stares. Most of the audience was made up of senior publishers and editors. They did not and in fact would never understand digital, let alone mobile. Ever the evangelist for a good idea, I kept going with my presentation, confident that I could turn them. However, I was not getting through. It was 2009, and the reality of technology advancement was not yet a priority—and with good reason.

Even with 2010 quickly approaching, smartphone penetration was just starting to take off. It would take several more years to reach critical mass. Yet, I kept at it in numerous boardrooms across the globe, and executive after executive refuted my proposals to mobile activate print for new revenue. They highlighted the lack of penetration as though it would be a decade or more before smartphones would really be in the hands of every person. As we all know, phones have zoomed past these expectations. Never have we seen a technology reach this level of market coverage as quickly as smart mobile did. But no matter; executives refused to pay attention to their biggest asset—readers—and the fact that a smartphone was in virtually every reader's hand with the potential to unlock new revenue, quickly.

By early 2011, if they weren't questioning smartphone penetration, the publishing executives I was dealing with were actually skeptical of apps. Many in the print industry thought consumers would never take the time to download the app needed to engage QR codes or augmented reality (whatever that was at the time). Of course, reading this now, you probably think I'm making this up. Not many people had really experienced an "app" until early 2011 and were even more skeptical that if someone downloaded an app, the user would use it enough to make it worth investing in and developing one. I was the laughingstock of the publishing industry.

WHEN ACTIVATING MOBILE, ACTIVATE THE EDITORIAL CONTENT FOR NEW REVENUE

So let's move to the present time: billions and billions of apps have now been downloaded. We are also well aware of the ever-increasing propensity for consumers to download apps, as 2012 had the distinction of being the year in which half of all apps to this point were downloaded. Consumers are also spending much more time with apps when they need to engage with brands multiple times to complete common, everyday tasks or just to entertain themselves. Yet, we are just now seeing print magazines and newspapers discovering how to bring to life the content behind their print pages with emerging mobile enablers, such as augmented reality that can be baked into a publishing app and operate much like the pioneering QR technology.

When I made that presentation to the MPA a few years back, I knew I was going to have an uphill battle with the industry. Publishers viewed digital as pennies to their print advertising dollars. Mobile was not even registering on their revenue radar screens. The far more valuable video revenue also seemed too far off in the distance to pay much heed. So, I focused my attention and persuasion on the editors in the room who could view such technologies as QR codes and the emerging augmented reality as an opportunity to give them the ability to create new editorial content and experiences. Subsequently, with consumer adoption, these experiences could be turned into new forms of advertising and revenue. The publishing side would come around—quickly.

My proposition then and today is very simple. Start taking steps to mobile activate every page, and leverage the amazing reach for new revenue by bridging readers from physical to virtual experience, with mobile as the bridge. For example, food magazines should utilize mobile enablers like QR codes and augmented reality applications to bring how-to videos and recipes to mobile for consumers—advertisers will want to be part of the experience. Sports magazines can bring to life additional photos, videos, and editorial content that doesn't fit in the print pages. And celebrity magazines can bring to life red-carpet events, fashion runways, and spectacular parties that fans would want to view and share immediately. Of course, you can tell that video will be the medium most desired by consumers and advertisers, but it's still struggling to get the operational attention with print publishers. And, so we are clear, the greatest opportunity lies with the print publishers that are largely dependent on advertising or are brands themselves with catalogues, free-standing inserts, and direct mail.

Two leaders for mobile activation in the advertising-based print publishing world are *Men's Fitness* and *GQ* magazines. Both employ a scan technology from Aurasma that is owned by HP and falls in the augmented reality space. Each magazine has created its own app that readers can activate while flipping through the pages of the magazines. When readers see the symbol for either the *GQ* or *Men's Fitness* app, they can simply tap the app on their phone, hold the phone's camera lens over the corresponding page, and watch the magic happen by way of delivery of extended related content to the reader, typically in video form. It's really quite impressive and demonstrates the creativeness certain publishers are using to extend their editorial products to both readers and advertisers.

THE TIME IS GROWING DIRE FOR PRINT PUBLICATIONS TO CREATE MOBILE-ACTIVATED REVENUE

Many of you may be saying at this point that you know how to use the technology to drive engagement, but the industry is still not seeing what I would call robust adoption. I think many would argue in the advertising-based print world that they struggle, like advertisers, with what the experience should be like when you transfer readers from your print pages to mobile devices for accessing additional virtual content. Experience is critical, and it's not uncommon to have a difficult time getting it right, but there's no excuse for editors and publishers not to test and develop new revenue streams with mobile activation. Advertisers seem to be outpacing the magazines and newspapers they buy by infusing their own creative with mobile activation, and I'm fearful that opportunity is starting to pass publishers by.

I guess what's most shocking about the print business is that despite the significant investments that have been poured into digital properties, traffic levels to websites where these properties reside fall well short of expectations relative to readership—even for the most popular magazines in the world. But Nellymoser found hope that print magazines are beginning to realize the value of mobile activation print pages. Their 2012 Mobile Survey of the top 100 magazines found a 61 percent increase in magazines using some form of mobile activation from Q1 to Q2 and a 107 percent growth trend year over year when comparing the same quarters. Even with this staggering growth, Nellymoser found that a majority of the scan codes were used by advertisers and hardly at all for the editorial content. The editors ignored it and the publishers drove a truck through it. We need more trucks, so to speak! Now is the time to create sponsor-worthy editorial opportunities.

The answer is quite simple, yet dire. The mobile activation of advertising-based print publishing needs to occur immediately. Print magazine and newspaper business hard-copy circulations are either stagnating or declining. Consumers are increasingly unwilling in a growing social world to pay for the most commoditized of content, including finance, sports, local news, weather, fashion, and other daily content. We are seeing circulation drops that are outstripping declines in advertising revenue, but this is sure to catch up as advertisers are drawn to more innovative ways to reach consumers with digital and mobile platforms.

Cash-strapped print publishers are downsizing everything from paper size to newsrooms. But we'll hit rock bottom when titles start disappearing at an alarming rate, and the amazing brand cache, audience reach, and once-large platforms for advertisers are squandered because mobile activation and the content to drive these experiences continue to be largely ignored.

HOW TO ACTIVATE DIGITAL FROM PRINT WITH MOBILE AS THE BRIDGE

The first place to start is an integrated mobile, print, and digital experience with the editorial content. If you are an editor at an entertainment magazine, there is no doubt that you probably have access to or are producing video every week that you can leverage in your pages. The mere act of social "liking" or "following" is now proof that consumers who love Kim Kardashian, One Direction, or Justin Bieber will follow them and seek out every piece of content—tweets, posts, videos, pics, written articles, or even audio—to stay close to them. I mean how could more than the 100 million people who collectively follow these stars be wrong, or at least be of no value?

Unlike any other media, print, especially magazines, is read in one hand with a phone typically within easy reach or held in the other. No other media—not even tablets or computers—have such dual usage. Plus, there's very complimentary content between print and the phone. For example, an interview with a famous figure may be absorbed in the magazine because of the amazing photos of the subject at home and on a recent red carpet event, but the reader can then be enticed in the editorial to see the full tour of their home or more of the interview video right on the phone.

Sharing is another reason to bring print and mobile together. We also know that if larger percentages of time are being spent with social networks via mobile devices, it's more likely that users will share content activated from print publications. Let's take an entertainment celebrity magazine, for example. By linking to video clips of top celebrities walking the red carpet, I can give the reader a sense of what it's like to be live in the moment or to share many more fashions on celebrities than I can otherwise feature on the pages of the magazine. Such a move can keep pace with other forms of both search and engagement. Current or archived forms of content—such as pictures and videos—can now be tapped for multiple purposes with advertisers covering related costs of new forms of content delivery.

Print publications also live or die by pass-along readership estimates. Pass-along readers are people who pick up a magazine and read it without having actually paid for it, such as when you pick up a magazine at the nail salon or dentist's office. The number of pass-along readers is usually estimated to be several multiples of people who subscribe and/or pay to receive the magazine. By activating print-to-video and other content with mobile, we can now create new forms of advertising for new revenue, especially from the pass-along readers. Then, the value of all print and virtual impressions grows because all platforms are working together to enrich the experience for the reader and advertiser.

The most immediate beneficiaries of taking active roles in linking print-to-video assets are the fashion, home improvement, food, and healthy lifestyle publications that have companion TV networks or shows, such as Esquire Network, HGTV, the Food Network, and

Dr. Oz. HGTV is probably the best example. Emanating out of the content found on the home improvement network and its shows, the magazine is one of the most successful new launches in a sea of decline. The pages of the magazine can come to life with do-it-yourself (DIY) video content that already exists from the thousands of hours of video footage from the TV network. By linking the two physical and virtual worlds with mobile as the bridge between the two, *HGTV* magazine could deliver a richer video experience to the consumer and expand its advertising inventory for brand partners.

Sue Kaufman adds this about *HGTV:* "Interesting that it can repurpose content it likely already has, or can obtain very cheaply. B-roll from event coverage, video cam footage from fashion shoots etc. This is very low cost, yet the opportunities in mobile to leverage are very high."

Advertisers also desire an integrated consumer experience and are ready to pay more for the opportunities. The historical organizational separation between the traditional print group and the mobile/digital group is often cited as an inefficiency in trying to build for this future. Every advertiser I have talked with recently was not only enthusiastic about integrating new forms of mobile activation with print and the new impressions it creates, but was also willing to pay much more for the opt-in, immersive, and data-driven experience it creates. Regardless of how the media businesses structure themselves or go after the advertising business, the advertisers want to see them working in concert together.

In fact, advertisers now outstrip the print publications they buy in mobile activation of their own ads. Pick up an average magazine and compare the ads to the editorial. I think you will find that the advertisers are more likely to prompt readers to take mobile action with QR codes, text codes, or even URLs to start a mobile experience right from their print ads. When advertisers are start-ing to advance farther than the print publications, the publications have a problem. Now, they are playing defense instead of offense, and they are leaving substantial sums of revenue on the table.

COMMITTING TO AND SELECTING AN ACTIVATION TECHNOLOGY

So, where do publishers and editors begin? First, they have to immediately integrate the capability to mobile activate the pages. Many options are emerging, especially in augmented reality. We have to be prepared for the fact that mobile activation is here to stay, and the ever-evolving technology to do so will now be a way of life for new engagement, revenue, and data. Dozens of technology enablers are cropping up to drive virtual experiences from print to the mobile phone. Picking one is a good first step. Committing editorial and sales resources to mobile activation is the next step. Being prepared to change it using space in a publication to market to the consumer every time you do will be a constant.

Aurasma, an augmented reality technology—altering a physi-cal space such as a magazine, newspaper, or movie poster—which HP bought, elevates scanning of print to a whole new level of virtual experience activated with the phone. According to *Wiki-pedia*, augmented reality is a live, copy, or view of a physical, real-world environment whose elements are augmented (or sup-plemented) by computer-generated sensory input such as sound, video, graphics, or GPS data. The Aurasma technology uses the phone's functions to scan and recognize the image in print—be it words or photos—and then takes you to an augmented experi-ence, such as video, music, more written content, images, and

other functions. The technology can be "white labeled" to magazine brands and housed within the brand's app, similar to how
Men's Fitness and *GQ* have used it. Editors and publishers alike
are drawn to this because they only have to market their own app
to readers to activate print pages, making it effective for the magazines to promote this and other features as simple for the users.
This technology advancement has the same principles as its older
sibling—the QR code—and delivers the same type of experience
by activating supporting video, delivering more written content,
or telling you about the author and allowing the user to share the
content of interest, among many other uses. There is little doubt
that as time unfolds more and more robust scan technologies will
be developed, and print publications simply need to set a course
for adopting this kind of activation right now.

MAKE THE ACTIVATIONS RELEVANT AND PURPOSE-DRIVEN

Video tends to be the most obvious feature to leverage from
print editorial and advertising. My partner Mark Berryhill,
who is a pioneer in branded video content and a co-founder
of the Video Solutions unit of mass publisher Meredith says,
"Publishers and print advertisers alike need to be very purpose
driven when creating a mobile activation that will drive to video
and other content. When I say purpose driven, I mean if you
are a food company, show me how to make that recipe. If you
are a home decor company, show me the latest trend in home
styles that features true design trends, not just your products.
The more your video and mobile experience helps the consumer,
the more the consumer will engage with your brands. It sounds

pedestrian, but in my experience, it's the most engaged content by pedestrians."

Let's take a look at some examples of purpose-driven content that piques the curiosity of readers and prompts them to engage with the additional content. For editorial coverage in a fashion magazine such as *GQ*, videos from the latest runway show or photos from the latest celebrity shoot can give readers added dimension to the clothes that are being advertised or show how they may look in movement. A celebrity magazine may consider featuring a video interview from which excerpts are pulled and included in the print article. A home magazine could allow the recipe for an editor's favorite meal to be downloaded to a phone for shopping, cooking, or learning. In all cases, we are delivering content that complements the written articles and takes the experience to a whole new level. It's also purpose driven because it's related naturally to what the content is and extends it to what readers are interested in.

Once you have chosen a mobile activation technology, you have to educate readers on how to use it and be sure it is getting liberal marketing and promotion space throughout the publication. *Men's Fitness* and *GQ* are expending significant space to educate consumers on how to use and get more with their mobile phones. In these cases, the magazines take their own space to advertise their named apps with instructions on how they work by telling readers to employ the apps and scan the page when they see an app symbol to activate an entire experience on their phone. The added bonus is that they are getting more web traffic from the print audience, which has proven challenging in the past for most print publishers. Relative to creating a better consumer experience, generating additional web traffic, and offering new advertising inventory, the cost for using "house" pages by publishers is relatively inexpensive and the online editorial teams are happy to shift resources to capture print readers—this is what they spend much of their day doing anyway.

Like with any new product, magazine publishers are very willing to expend inexpensive print real estate for promotion and activation of content even before they have advertisers, knowing that "if you build it, they will come." In the case of both *GQ* and *Men's Fitness*, some of the editorial that's activated does come with an advertiser. In addition, those magazines are starting to offer the advertisers the ability to apply mobile activation to their print ads throughout the magazine by way of promotion ads and a download index of advertisers. The publishers can then decide on an advertiser-by-advertiser basis if they want to charge separately for this feature or bundle it with a larger advertising package.

Next, start small. Pick just a few experiences to extend to the mobile phone. I have worked with some publications that have attempted to do too much both for the editorial staff and the reader and have ultimately failed because the efforts were too numerous and lacked focus. Start with small steps to educate and illuminate key pieces of editorial content. You may even consider creating a new index page for mobile downloads in every issue or just activating select content from select pages. Accompanying features created with or for advertisers should be kept to a minimum.

Once you've identified a few places to start activation, your mobile experience needs to keep pace with each publication's edition and be very simple for the consumer to navigate. Some campaigns just send readers to the publication's mobile app, but I prefer to send them directly to the specific web experience for the content promoted. For example, *Men's Fitness* makes its monthly fitness routines mobile activated, which is of high value to both consumers and advertisers. Why? Because of all the mobile devices out there, the one that is most easily portable in a gym environment is your phone. Having a new workout routine or exercise on your phone is valuable to the consumer and gives the integrated advertiser multiple impressions each time the user activates it. Plus, the editors can create a template for consistent sections or content, such as workout routines in the fitness publication, streamlining the process for uploading and activating content with each edition. In addition, the mobile app, which is usually intended to do much more than provide one piece of content or experience, can now more easily get additional page views from the user beyond the one or two content downloads that come from the magazine— online publishers tend to focus solely on increasing the number of page views, and thus advertising impressions and revenue.

INTEGRATE THE OPERATIONS, DON'T CONTINUE TO SEPARATE THEM

To offer an integrated experience from print to mobile to digital destinations as well as advertising offerings, you have to work together within organizations—no more silos. New forms of editorial mobile activation will lead to new forms of advertising inventory and brand integration. Yet, many businesses are still operating under the assumption that print, digital, and video— along with emerging mobile—should all be disconnected with separate sales teams, editorial teams, marketing teams, compensation schemes, and of course, P&Ls. Just like mobile signals penetrate the walls of your office, we have to find ways to break through the walls of our organizations.

CHAPTER 7: THUMB'S UP TIPS

- Many publishers have made tablet investments, but few have done the same with mobile, even as its penetration has skyrocketed in the last two years. Now's the time to begin mapping the strategies and implementing the plans.

- Leverage your richest assets—readership and the data that comes with it. Use mobile to extend, leverage, and grow this asset.

- Break down the silos between print, digital, and video. Stop viewing the print product as the end game and start making the transition to leveraging it as the means to the end. Integrate, integrate, integrate: we have got to bring all of these pieces together with integrated experiences: editorial, sales, and new compensation models that err on collaboration instead of easy financial documentation.

- Mobile activation is here to stay, and the ever-evolving technology to do so will now be a way of life for new engagement, revenue, and data.

- Pick a mobile activation technology that is right for your publication and market it significantly to your readers and advertisers. Start with small steps of just a few activations to educate internal and external audiences, and illuminate key pieces of editorial content.

- Spend as much time as needed on ensuring that the mobile experience is as high quality as the print page design, quality, and experience. The mobile experience needs to keep pace with each publication's edition and be very simple for the consumer to navigate.

CHAPTER 8

Impulse Buy!

Retail Shelves Come Alive

REINVENTING THE ONE FORM OF MARKETING IN CONSTANT REINVENTION—RETAIL

There is probably no older form of marketing than that found within the four walls of a retail establishment or immediately outside it. The industry has worked actively to evolve retail marketing, whether conceiving novel marketing plans like in-store TV networks (that have really never taken off) or floor decals in front of shelves telling you about a new product (other than peripheral vision, does anyone really look at the floor while shopping?). Regardless of their limited success, these channels certainly command new forms of shelf and marketing allowances from vendors primarily due to the increase in product

competition. However, mobile may just be the most innovative opportunity for retail, shelf, and product marketing from
advancing sales to customer loyalty.

To understand how mobile can advance even the most forward thinking of retailers, I would like to highlight one of my
favorites. Trader Joe's is a unique retailer that has sprung up in
markets where no analyst or lender thought competition in the
stodgy grocery retail space was possible. It came on the scene with
its fun, kitschy, Southern California surfer shop motif, offering
really good grocery and ready-to-eat frozen items at rock-bottom
prices. I will often spend no more than $60 at Trader Joe's, but
I'll come away with 10 days' worth of meals or more. They are
a recession darling by appealing to consumers with high quality,
low prices, flavors that keep pace with trends; they are growing
like gangbusters with diverse, younger consumers and thus proving themselves the perfect retailer to lead on mobile.

The Trader Joe's I frequent in Manhattan is busy from the
time it opens until the time it closes, with check-out lines that
move swiftly but still encircle the entire perimeter of the store.
Despite the lines—and to ensure I don't miss a thing I need—I
shop all interior aisles first and then get in line to pay, knowing that I will shop the perimeter aisles as I wait. While waiting
patiently in this creative retail environment, I began to think
about the possibilities of mobile and retail coming together.

Mobile marketing is not new to Trader Joe's. It was one of
the first specialty grocery retailers with a targeted mobile advertising effort that promoted the portions of its site containing store
locations, recipes, and other offers. According to *Mobile Marketer* associate editor Rimma Kats, at the time TJ's announced

its campaign, she applauded its effort by saying, "Running a targeted [mobile] ad campaign that's really effective for [Trader Joe's] because its consumers are always on the street and have their mobile device in hand. When it serves an ad with recipes for tonight, people are going to be more inclined to tap on it." So, Trader Joe's is really thinking about mobile with purpose-driven content and has already started down the path of highlighting its popular foods in easy-to-make recipes. Now is the time for Trader Joe's and other retailers to consider how to take this to the next level.

Here's one example of taking it to the next level. In looking around the store from the checkout line, it struck me that Trader Joe's not only shook up the retail world by pioneering a mobile advertising campaign on Pandora—a music app that is free on the phone and one of the most popular—but it's also pushing the in-store marketing envelope with its fun, sardonic marketing messages scrolled in vintage cartoon script on balloon cut-outs above relevant displays of food. This is where the mobile campaign can go to the next level by combining physical display marketing with the same recipe tips in the store that are activated with the mobile campaign out of store. While the in-store marketing is very retro to the point of being completely outmoded, this is where I got to thinking that mobile activation of these displays could really elevate Trader Joe's and really any retailer's or consumer product's (CPG's) game. Once in a retail environment, the hardest selling is done. Since I am now in the store, the goal for any retailer is to get me to put additional ("impulse") items in the cart by giving me more ideas for using products and to entice me with cost-saving messages as I go to check out.

Some of the displays embody the personality of Trader Joe's but also could lend themselves to marketing activation such as, "Try Our Greek Yogurt in Healthy Stuffed Potatoes," "What the Kale Is Kale?" and "Shea It Ain't So Dry Skin." These little messages and tips are the perfect "starters" for activation with my mobile for instant viewing of the answers while I wait to pay (on average about 12 to 15 minutes), or I could bookmark related recipes, videos, social connections, and tips for when I need them later at home. The mobile activation of additional information displayed on shelves could motivate me to put additional items in my cart that I didn't intend to buy when I entered the store— the ultimate goal of all in-store marketing. As any good retailer knows, once I am in-store the cost of each additional product sale has gone down appreciably. Any new items the in-store marketing could prompt me to buy just doesn't drop to the bottom of my cart. In large part, it drops to the retailer's bottom line. For very little investment, mobile activation could not only reinvent a category, it could also propel a far greater return than any other form of in-store marketing the retail sector has ever seen.

WITH MOBILE, IN-STORE CAN DRIVE NEW E-COMMERCE SALES

In-store displays are still the untapped frontier in mobile marketing and e-commerce. We always have our phones on us, even while shopping in-store. Many of us also store our grocery lists, recipes for the week, and coupon offers right on our phones. Linking the visual displays in-store to the mobile devices of shoppers could promote impulse buys or links to mobile sites for more product options. This may sound perverse in logic, as many retailers are trying to drive in-store traffic and sales with in-store mobile use, but e-commerce is a force to be reckoned with and presents opportunities for an ongoing buying relationship that extends beyond the store. According to statistics, a vast majority of us go online to seek deals before shopping. According to the GMA/Booz & Company Shopper Survey in 2013, 62 percent of shoppers searched for deals digitally, including mobile, for at least half of their shopping trips to stores. Sure, we all still actively indulge in impulse buys, but these purchases are often done with some online knowledge of price. Most bulk, repeated, or expensive items are going to be priced online before buying. This is a phenomenon that's here to stay, so don't fight it, go with it. The question is, how?

Cosmetic companies, especially those with higher price points, probably have the hardest time with the "embrace the e-commerce wave" advice. One of the biggest complaints from companies relying on physical store sales is that many people will stop by the displays in a department store for such freebies as samples, makeovers, or product advice, but they indicate that they will search the web in the hopes of finding a lower price instead of buying in-store. These companies—such as cosmetics— continue to live and die by in-store profits, and the more upscale the cosmetics and perfumes, the more the business is dependent on the "live" experience. In the days before online buying proliferated, companies could tie their in-store budgets for such labor-intensive practices as makeovers to the average sale returned from products used during those sessions. Those days are long gone. Regardless of these tried-and-true methods, many beauty companies are seeing in-store sales drop while seeing a rise in online sales—they know the marketing is working, but they just don't know how.

Our company has been approached by friends who happen to design and build in-store displays for some of the biggest cosmetic and perfume retailers. They came to us for help in deploying solutions for getting customers to buy on the spot, or at least track the consumer's path to purchase on a retailer's site or on other competing, lower-cost sites. The biggest struggle is that they are working within a retail category that is probably the most searched online to find savings before shopping.

Curtailing consumer online shopping behavior is not the goal, yet inventing new reasons for the consumer to engage with cosmetic and retail brands in the store is critical. Mobile can actually help this strategy. One obvious area to leverage is utilizing the video content beauty brands produce by providing customers with up-close fashion trends and "how-to-get-the-look" tips. Even if customers come into the store for complete makeovers, the kiosks could give out mobile-activated postcards with text or scan codes for how to achieve the same look they got in the store days later when they want to apply it again at home on their own. The kiosks provide customized content and the online activation gives customers a reason to go back and shop at their leisure. This allows the cosmetic company to offer related products at either the retailer or other preferred outlets at prices that match the lowest on the web.

Sue Kaufman, who has led efforts serving such CPG brands as Campbell's while at Y&R and Group M, says this about the opportunities for in-store: "The problem for all hard consumer goods, especially cosmetics and electronics, is the consumer goes to the store to see it, try it, and then goes online to buy it. Best Buy is doing a good job of combating this by embracing it. It brags that the stores are WiFi enabled and invite you to comparison shop on your phone right in their own store. Or two stores in my UWS Manhattan side neighborhood have taken a different tack. One of them has posted a sign stating that anyone caught taking pictures of the tags will be asked to leave. The other one works on guilt, with a sign that states 'Love the Upper West Side? Prove it. Shop local.'"

Another way to get customers to buy more through the brand and retailer is to offer automatic reorder at discounted rates—especially for goods that are used frequently, such as dark spot correctors and moisturizers, or for a fresh selection of seasonal colors automatically delivered at the start of each quarter. Just as the industry advanced the "bonus" buying opportunities, we need to advance features that allow marketing to the consumer long after they leave the store, even if the store is the only place they discovered the cosmetic products.

THE PERSONAL TOUCH—UNLEASHING NEW MOBILE OPPORTUNITIES

Cosmetic, clothing, and other retailers are unique in the sense that consumers tend to get friendly with the sales staff over time and multiple, repeated shopping trips. Most brand managers cite the importance of having good customer relations both with the local retail management and between the retail management and consumer. Thinking about your habits, there are likely salespeople and service providers—from your hair stylist to a department store cosmetician to a manager at your local grocery store—who have transcended the sales roles and become de facto style consultants with deep knowledge of your tastes, preferred colors, and sizes for different items. There is much opportunity for brands and retailers to now leverage these relationships and make them accessible with the advancements in mobile communications. Mobile now allows companies to create even deeper customer touchpoints that were not possible before. Loyalty programs of all types, such as rewards cards and mobile chats with sales personnel when they are on duty but you can't get to them in person, will benefit from mobile advancements. Those efforts likely will result in online orders.

Whether you've just bought shoes from a salesperson or you shop regularly at an online store, you have much better opportunities through mobile to have more personal experiences with the company. Amazon is advancing this concept by using pop-up sales consultants with whom you can instant message, and retailers with physical locales can also consider doing the same by taking real-time communications technology such as Facetime® and other similar live video communications platforms enterprise wide. Such platforms can make local personnel available when they are on duty, but on a virtual basis because they are interacting with consumer regardless of where they are in time or place. For department stores, having a 24/7 style consultant available can provide advice and online sales for when consumers need it most—on the night of a big date, the day of your daughter's wedding, a company picnic, or just those little everyday events where you need some help to look your best. Just like friends, good sales and personal services folks constantly receive text messages and e-mails from customers seeking help. Maybe it's now time to embrace face-to-face, instant technologies to formally stretch these relationships outside of the four walls of a retail store, and also to accompany the communications with easy-to-buy applications to turn advice into instant sales—never occurring, but certainly starting in-store.

Major toy manufacturers with strong retail presence enable many of their products with "try me" buttons. Because toys make such a unique sound, we can employ audio detection technologies such as Shazam or scan codes to deliver an in-store mobile experience instantly to complement the shopping decision process. The brand could deliver product information and reviews for specific toys, instant gift requests, and the ability to add to "wish lists," savings offers, and even free content such as games, apps, or videos, among many other options to spur purchases. Regardless of the product type you are selling in a store, I am confident that if you sat down for just a few minutes and thought of ways to further engage the consumer on mobile from the product or displays themselves, you can come up with ideas that would form the basis of the experience you will now build.

CREATING THE RIGHT MOBILE EXPERIENCE TAKES RETAIL INGENUITY

Even if companies are embracing mobile activation in retail advertising, we find that today's brands—large and small—want to send customers off to a single web experience that seems to be "one size fits all," but is not tailored to either the current campaign or the mindset or purchase intentions of the in-store and window-shopping consumers. Going back to our toy example, we need to put on our "situational marketing" hat and think about the mindset of a hurried mom in the toy store the night before her child's birthday party or in the few days before a major holiday. It is critical to create a mobile experience that will be embraced by consumers and help the shopping process when there's little attention or time, or a strain on budgets.

To help build this experience, it often will simply require that a brand's team look at existing assets that have been used for other marketing activities and bring them to the retail point of sale with the capability of mobile. Video assets are one prime example that could hasten a purchase decision, but may not be employed at the retail level. At a previous time, my partner Mark produced do-it-yourself (DIY) videos that ended up just sitting, waiting to be discovered, on a home improvement store's website. The videos were not really connected to the tens of millions of people visiting the stores each week, yet mobile presented the opportunity to do it and maybe inspire a whole new set of customers with ideas delivered with the efficiency and effectiveness of video.

Working with the same home improvement retailer and several vendors, we proposed an in-store network of DIY videos that would be mobile activated right on the shelves next to relevant products. The DIY content already existed, so it was relatively easy and cost-effective to create the promotion and pair the videos with the products on shelves. We prepared tests intended for several stores, placed shelf-talkers with three ways to download the content—QR codes (the highest engaged), text codes, or old-fashioned URLs—depending on what customers were most comfortable with. We created a very simple navigation to all the videos, but ensured that the video requested always popped to the top of the menu and automatically played. The videos were no more than five minutes in length and showed customers how to do basic things such as tile a floor, put up wallpaper, replace a toilet, and plant a garden.

THE HOLY GRAIL OF RETAILERS GROWS WITH MOBILE—DATA AND SHELF-ALLOWANCES

This home improvement retailer also found that with mobile it could expand the data it captured on individual shoppers, their interests, and what was going into their carts. The store was even able to offer favorable financing terms with the bigger projects via mobile, as well as extend credit card offers on the video menu, so it could capture consumer information on the spot and for future marketing.

Mobile is a natural extension of the traditional shelf allowance. In our retail example of DIY videos, several major vendors also asked to pay for the privilege to appear in the videos, helping to curtail the cost of future video production. John Ross, a former big box CMO and CEO of Shopper Sciences and now Executive Vice President at Inmar Technologies, has told me that in research he's reviewed, a vast majority of people will buy a brand ingredient if the brand is listed in a recipe—such as a video. Home-improvement retailers and vendors would welcome a fraction of this majority, especially if it meant expanding the average basket to more items as a result of mobile activation of DIY videos in-store or online. To further impact the mobile experience, vendors could also have a 30-second spot before the DIY video and have their logo or special savings offers appear in the retailer's mobile experience. This is an interesting but not surprising development in the use of mobile in everyday shopping, and it could expand the revenue that retailers receive from vendors for appearing in videos and other mobile experiences, offsetting the cost of video production and activation. Our initial tests with retailers were very successful and many retailers are starting to expand and experiment with new forms of mobile activation, tapping the same content and shopping experiences they have been producing for years.

In the same vein, we recently produced three videos for Burnett's flavored vodkas. The company was seeking to promote some of its holiday flavors with a video showing how easy it is to make cocktails using their liquor. The videos would be used in the lifestyle segments of our daily TV show and would be given to Burnett's to be used on social, web, and in-store displays, if they chose. While all other forms of marketing are key in the liquor space, in-store is where I actually think the biggest opportunity exists because of the large amount of foot traffic, especially among novice holiday party hosts seeking ideas and advice for their celebrations. Mobile activation can also add tremendous value and interaction with the already costly in-store displays. But how could this be done?

The target demographic for Burnett's is young adults who are adept with mobile, so there are several options to get users to download in-store helpful entertaining content, such as how-to-make videos. Scan codes are obvious means for mobile activation and can be applied to the print display and call-outs to get how-to-make videos; or if there is less shelf space, the technology as simple as that found in musical greeting cards can be applied to shelf hangers. The consumer is prompted with shelf hanger messages to press the picture representing their favorite holiday song, which is then picked up by the Shazam app on the consumer's phone and delivers a mobile experience triggered by it. With each mobile path, consumers are able to unlock great recipes and party ideas, and even enter contests or download free music. (For those who work for or with liquor companies: of course the first screen should be an age verification page.)

These are just a few of the ideas where mobile can enhance the in-store experience by tapping existing content and features customized by product, department, or geography. Salespeople can also spark sales by transcending the physical space as virtual mobile consultants and friends. Most importantly, we were able to do many of these strategies cost effectively and with performance that pays for itself very quickly. Mobile really does give "impulse buy" an entirely new meaning, and may also start to provide new types of shelf allowances and co-marketing around the creation of video and other forms of useful content.

With each in-store experience, you have to consider what consumers are doing and thinking and what is prompting them to buy. In many cases, a single web experience will not work for all of these audiences, especially in an outdoor or in-store environment. You want to provide enough specific and relevant information for consumers to make a purchase now.

CHAPTER 8: THUMB'S UP TIPS

- Even physical retailers can benefit from mobile technology. If you are primarily focused on in-store or on-site sales, embrace e-commerce and think about ways to link both the virtual and physical worlds using the customer and their phones as the bridge.

- In-store displays are still largely untapped opportunities. Look at your displays both in-store/on-site and on the storefront for how you would activate.

- With geolocation, retailers can increase and vendors can actually reverse the shelf-allowance model by pointing consumers directly to the retailer's e-commerce site or to a preferred retailer, which may be offering greater incentives.

- Why are your customers in your store rather than online? What information would they like right now about your product? What would get them to buy now or even later, long after they have left? Is the answer recipes, how-to videos, coupons, automatic re-orders, immediate price matching with online vendors, or adding their friendly sales rep to favorites for consultation?

- With emerging audio-detection technologies such as Shazam, we could deliver to the consumer's mobile phone in-store product information and reviews, instant gift requests for an upcoming birthday or holiday gift, savings offers, and even free content such as games, apps, or videos to spur purchases.

- Most brands that have a street-side or in-store presence have also invested heavily in applications—many of which are free—but lack awareness even among their most loyal consumers. Just the omnipresent availability of these apps with every mobile experience will greatly enhance the likelihood of download and engagement.

- While in-store, the mobile activation of additional information—videos, how-tos, recipes, tips to bookmark, coupon savings, ordering out of stock items—could motivate consumers to put additional items in their carts that they didn't intend to buy when they entered the store—the ultimate goal of all in-store marketing.

- Consider how best to activate mobile, whether inside or outside the store. Many brands are using QR codes, text codes, and even music/sound-activated technologies such as Shazam to drive interaction and begin or continue the sales relationship, even and especially when the consumer departs the store. Many enablers are easy to find and some are even free (if you don't mind ads with your content).

- Many local buyers consider salespeople family—whether it is the dry cleaner or the cosmetician at their favorite store. These salespeople tend to transcend the sales process and become de facto style consultants and even friends. It's now time to embrace face-to-face, instant technologies to formally stretch these relationships outside of the walls of a retail store and also accompany the communications with easy-to-buy applications to turn advice into instant sales—never occurring, but certainly starting in-store.

CHAPTER 9

Out-of-Home Becomes Relevant Again

"OUT-OF-HOME" IS TRADITIONALLY DEFINED AS any advertising that we see while outside of our houses, such as billboards or display boards in subways, airports, or movie theaters. The out-of-home sector has also worked to shed its image as purveyors of eyesore billboards by attempting to change their industry moniker to such kitschy titles as "play space media" (which I guess refers to every place outdoors being a "playground") but also innovating with video billboards. The latter still draw the scorn of regulators because of the distraction to drivers—locally and nationally—but they certainly take advantage of the ever-progressing "jumbotron" television evolution. It is still shocking to see how crisp and true-to-life these large screens are becoming from the roadside boards to those in stadiums. In all instances, the out-of-home marketing and advertising industry has really failed to catapult itself beyond intrusiveness, but there are glimmers of hope, and mobile can help deliver the opportunities.

By now you are realizing that mobile opportunities can be seen in every facet and movement of my day, especially in the most traditional and local forms of marketing. So it's not surprising that the biggest opportunities for mobile are in play space media. Regardless of what you call it, nothing beats the opportunity to drive awareness and impulse buys at the foot, street, and retail traffic levels. I am not just an observer of out-of-home marketing, I am a participant in it.

WINDOW SHOPPING BECOMES MOBILE SHOPPING

Repeatedly, we hear from politicians and economists alike that small businesses drive both our economy and employment. The same holds true for spending on marketing and advertising by businesses, especially locally, where we often see innovation rise from the "street level," such as those who own businesses like restaurants or "mom-and-pop" shops.

I own several small businesses, including a stake in an inn and restaurant in a highly seasonal tourist destination. When my partners and I opened the businesses in late 2009, we experimented with QR codes to simply get people to like our Facebook page. I made up flyers with codes, framed them, and placed them in high-traffic areas of the restaurant that said, "If you like us, scan this code and show it on our Facebook page." It really did the trick. People scanned the code and our "likes" increased, bolstering our presence on Facebook. I couldn't understand why I constantly heard skepticism back in New York from advertisers on scan codes, yet as a marketer myself—small-time as we may be—I saw the magic firsthand.

As you walk by the many restaurants, shops, galleries, and boutiques that make up your town, imagine the amazing opportunities to encourage consumers to mobile activate menus, reservations, e-commerce, and videos promoting daily events. Then, think about the big brands that also rely on this form of marketing. They have equal opportunities to leverage both foot and store traffic and with even more resources. Yet, for some reason, mobile has not yet fully invaded these areas of the most common and highest-spending forms of marketing.

Most small retailers—of which many are still owned by individuals or families—can take small, yet meaningful steps toward establishing a 24/7 mobile marketing presence just outside of their establishments or in local marketing materials. They can add mobile activation to menus, window displays, and business-card–sized ads in weekly community newspapers with QR codes or the retailer's very own five-digit text code. Both are relatively easy to establish, and are similar to getting a phone number or a web address, but with some cost and feature differences. Microsoft is my preferred provider of QR codes, which you can find underneath their mobile products and, unless you are going to use these in heavy commercial purposes, are relatively inexpensive and easily changeable. Microsoft makes it relatively straightforward to get your own code and then link it to any URL or web destination you want. Plus, you have the ability to change it as many times as you want and as often as you want. Text codes or short codes can also be obtained through providers like Veri-sign. These take a little longer to establish and can cost anywhere from a few thousand per year to $10,000 or more, depending on the features. Once you have decided which way to go, you want to use it as a chance to showcase the parts of your business that will drive the highest sales, whether it's your award-winning food, amazing service, stunning views, good prices, or fashion-able designs.

George Kliavkoff, who runs Hearst's Ventures arm and is co-president of its Entertainment and Syndication division, says this about the renewed importance of local businesses with respect to emerging mobile phone data: "Of all the sensors in the phone that have only been available, the primary one has been the GPS. This is important for businesses that rely on local foot or street traffic, because we can now target search ads, and others, based on someone's location."

And he's also optimistic about the technological growth in the number and expanded detection of sensors in the phone that brands can use to deliver valuable services and relevant messages. "Now, we are seeing new sensors in the phones that throw off data such as the accelerometer [detecting speed of a consumer whether on foot, bike, or motor] proximity detector [telling when the consumer moves even a few feet, at the moment they do it] and soon, the thermometer and barometer [for health, weather changes] . . . There's a class of entrepreneurs that will cre-ate really interesting businesses sitting on top of the data that comes from all these and other sensors. And, some will be in the health and life sciences, retail spaces, services area, and almost by definition most of these businesses will be local in nature."

As such, most of the businesses that employ out-of-home advertising are local in nature. This opportunity to tap these interactions between this type of advertising and mobile has never been greater, especially for those marketers who have foresight about the vast mobile capacity for local data that now exists.

DISPLAY BOARDS CAN BECOME MOBILE BOARDS IN ONE TAP

While they may seem like they are just taking up space, billboards on highway exit ramps can actually be the most impactful marketing. Just think how many times you rely on them to find gas, restrooms, food, outlets, and a night's stay in unfamiliar areas. Certainly, billboards have seen very little innovation. Video and HD billboards were some of the most recent advancements in outdoor advertising, but are now coming under fire from consumer groups and government entities alike because they represent distractions to drivers and pedestrians. Furthermore, advertisers still put phone numbers, URLs, and QR codes on their outdoor and transit marketing materials, even though most people pass them too quickly or won't be able to connect fast enough.

Probably the most extreme example of lacking innovation in outdoor advertising occurs at the transit hub or station level, where consumers are primarily on their feet and WiFi is starting to proliferate, aiding mobile activation. Despite this, transit advertisers are largely overseen by stodgy government entities, which never really think innovatively about advertising nor do we expect them to advance advertising in space they control. So, as a result, government entities are looking for revenue literally in every corner of their public facilities and often will "create" revenue with new billboards added to every corner.

Walk through any train station or airport these days and you will see free-standing mini-billboards popping up in the middle of sidewalks, airport aisles, at the tops of stairs, and even at gate check-in areas. Some advertisers are now employing video and sound to get your attention as though their immobile, fixed positions in the middle of your walkway weren't enough of an obstruction. I guess the philosophy is that you can't avoid running into them, and transport authorities are all happy to oblige these new forms of inventory for the revenue. So while obtrusive and certainly unavoidable, it's become a way of life in this up-and-down global economy. If we have to live with these new innovations at eye level, it's time to think about how to make these mobile activated.

Similar to billboards, menu boards, as well as window and free-standing displays for small business shops, restaurants, and other establishments, rely on foot traffic and impulse entry to drive revenue. In our restaurant and inn, a good 50 percent of the traffic that enters our establishment to eat, drink, and maybe stay overnight are individuals who stopped to review the menu board and posted specials. Their discovery of us and decision to become our patrons are intricately linked and almost instantaneous.

In many ways, the traveler is a target for advertisers who deliver messages on boards whether in airports or in destinations such as where we have the restaurant. As such, restaurants, live entertainment, hotels, and tours are often the ones you see most, whether advertised to mass audiences in train stations or to those pedestrians that pass by your business—even when closed. For the many of us who rely on foot traffic—such as restaurants and bars—what can we do to remind potential customers about us for their next meal or get-together, detail our specials, bring to life our menu, or even to make online reservations when they are in a rush or easily distracted by the next storefront? In my opinion, small and large business owners have to think about their storefronts as 24/7 billboards that can become active advertisements with mobile phones. It is relatively inexpensive to build apps that can be easily updated to support your business. But I also find that having a simple, mobile-optimized website that can be easily changed is the best route to go.

MAKING MOBILE YOUR 24/7 SALESPERSON

Taking action is what we strive for in marketing. Placing a QR code, text code, or some other form of mobile activation may actually facilitate more interaction. Perusing the big outdoor advertising vendors as well as the non-savvy small shop owners, I see very little innovation being offered in the way of mobile and it will be up to the advertisers to bring their creativity to mobile activation.

With regard to evolving out of home marketing, we are always working with limitations inherent in the medium. Billboards are definitely on a set schedule, which makes tailoring messages, let alone changing them, difficult and costly in anything less than 30 days. The same holds true for small shop owners who can't change their marketing materials quickly due to lack of time, available funds, or both. Sure, while video and high-definition boards, especially at the foot-traffic level, allow for more frequent content updates, it is still difficult to change and tailor messages for the wide variety of people in your average airport, train terminal, or on Main Street. However, mobile screens and experiences can be updated on a second-by-second basis with just a change in the URL to which they point.

So a restaurant, for example, may focus on the attractiveness of the bar for after-work drinks, encouraging patrons from a display board to see inside the bar without going in or even being near it. This can be done by providing a URL, text code, or scan code. Another establishment may attract with happy hour specials starting at $4. The restaurant manager can decide to establish specials each day for $4 without specifying or worrying about changing the board for each day's specials, which could vary based on ingredient availability or the specialties of different chefs on shift. No more information has to be conveyed other than encouraging potential patrons to scan a code and see today's $4 specials right on their phone. While the specials may change, the restaurant can simply update its website and the mobile experience will change along with it. Marketers large and small can also add "mobile specials"—such as a room or car upgrade, additional percentage off a meal, or added bonus with purchase—for those who take the time to engage.

Sue Kaufman, director of channel planning at Y&R, also has this to say: "It's hard to discuss this without bringing in data collection and remarketing. The actual action may not be related to the experience, such as a menu on the phone, as I don't need to see the menu when I'm already sitting in the restaurant. But if you entice me to download content and get my e-mail address [perhaps with a coupon savings] then you can remind me when what I ordered is on special again, etc., as well as requesting me to review in Yelp and more."

Another simple example of this occurred while I was waiting in line at a movie theater. The call to action in a poster for an upcoming film encouraged me to watch the trailer by scanning the displayed code. It would also let me download an associated mobile game for free in exchange for my e-mail address, giving me the chance to be entertained by the movie content even before the movie came out. The potential result is multiple repeat impressions that could ultimately tempt me to go see the film. However, the most valuable aspect was acquiring my e-mail address for re-marketing the movie closer to its premiere date, as well as other movies the studio is releasing down the road.

Recently, I was in a McDonald's buying breakfast. There was nothing outstanding about its use of mobile that was obvious to me in the store. I picked up my purchase, which was neatly placed in a paper bag they have used for years and I was on my way. Once I got back to my hotel room, I discovered a scan code about half the size of my coffee on the outside of the bag. I was stunned. Here McDonald's was realizing that I, like many customers, was probably sitting alone, phone in hand, about to indulge my taste buds, and they took advantage by marketing to me on the bag. I scanned the code and found a variety of menu items, job openings, and other interesting tidbits. Now here was a world-class example of taking an old form of out-of-home marketing and creating a whole mobile experience to accompany my meal.

ENTICING ENCORES AREN'T THE ONLY
USE FOR MOBILE AT CONCERTS

Concerts also provide a great opportunity to reach people of a common demographic, or at least of common interests. However, as today's mobile technology has advanced, so too have the concerns of concert promoters and artists that their intellectual property will be compromised by Facetime or other streaming services.

Recently, my kids and I were at a well-known band's concert that was being sponsored by Farmers Insurance. Part of the venue was standard area seating, and the other part was a great lawn where you could throw out a blanket and sit where you wanted. My 18-year-old had friends who were also attending and he wanted the chance to roam a bit with them. He quickly realized that the mobile signals were disabled. When we inquired with a security guard, he confirmed that mobile signals are "contained" to prevent people from exploiting the show for money.

Seriously?

Pushing aside my concerns for my children's and others' safety as reason enough for not disabling or "containing" signals, I began to wonder about Farmers Insurance—they kept playing messages encouraging fans to tweet a certain hashtag for the chance to win seat upgrades right on the spot. The problem? No one could get to Twitter, and the concert management was likely perplexed at the lack of activity, at least from anyone in the venue. More importantly, the advertiser had a great idea to engage fans and endear them to the brand, but the experience became frustrating and had the exact opposite effect. Concert goers sitting around us were mystified and actually blamed Farmers Insurance for the failed experience.

Even if it did work, I wondered why the insurer picked Twitter in what would be just a one-way exchange. I'm sure their goal was for people to request quotes for their varied insurance needs. Why not post a text code so you could get a two-way interaction going with the consumer? Most would not have won the seat upgrade, but maybe Farmers could have instantly offered the chance to win an all-expense-paid trip to the location of the end-of-tour concert just for calling to get an insurance estimate. Or they could have provided an instant quote via mobile by asking a few questions about the vehicles and drivers in the hope of converting someone who was thinking about changing insurers. The ability to create a mobile relationship with a fan at a live venue is probably one of the greatest opportunities that exists for brands that sponsor; however, the extreme lack of control, as pointed out, makes it a high-risk marketing tactic.

On top of the brand opportunities, there was the lost opportunity for the artists, concert organizers, and record labels to sell merchandise and maybe even deliver it right to a fan's seat. I went several times during the concert to buy a t-shirt and other band-branded goods, only to be turned away by the lines that snaked around the venue. I had $100 burning a hole in my pocket just for the purpose and it never got spent. What if I were met with signs that simply showed a text code and said, "Why wait in line? Order what you want, when you want and we will have it waiting for you when you leave the concert or sent to your home!" You could only imagine the kinds of add-on goods and services that could be offered in this way, not to mention the advertising positions sold to the insurance company sponsor or others.

OUT-OF-HOME HAS THE ABILITY TO
GET VERY PERSONAL AND SOCIAL

One of the greatest opportunities for activating outdoor and in-store experiences is the geotargeting data that gets unlocked at the most personal of levels. With consumer permission, we can ascertain much more information about who's buying, the type of phone they are using, the type of content they are engaging (demonstrating their interests for future experience development), and, of course, what's prompted them to buy either now or later. Nothing, in my opinion, from a data-analysis perspective, presents the kind of opportunities that we are seeing with geo-local targeting at the mobile phone level, especially with out-of-home marketing.

Most brands that have a street-side or in-store presence have also invested heavily in applications—many of which are free—but lack awareness even among their most loyal of consumers. Just simply having these apps available as an omnipresent feature with every mobile experience will greatly enhance the likelihood of download and engagement.

Social is the next obvious winner in geotargeting with outdoor marketing, allowing those who have just experienced a brand to instantly like it or give feedback on a poor experience, allowing the company to immediately take appropriate action either way. It could come in the form of a 20-percent-off coupon for your friends or followers, encouraging them to bring a friend the next time. Or, if there was a negative experience, it allows the brand to react in real time, letting customers know their review was received and offering to rectify their error or give it another try. I have learned—especially in our restaurant business—that just recognizing and responding to consumer grievances can help make fans out of the most ardent of complainers.

With geolocation, vendors like cosmetic companies, toy manufacturers, or hotel chains can actually reverse the shelf-allowance model and point consumers directly to their e-commerce site or to a preferred retailer that may be offering greater incentives. With mobile activation, every brand becomes a media channel to market. It's how we direct it and facilitate it that will make the difference.

Hopefully, these mobile ideas are inspiring those of you looking to transcend your out-of-home and retail experiences.

CHAPTER 9: THUMB'S UP TIPS

- Small and large business owners have to think about their storefronts as 24/7 billboards that are active advertisements with the mobile phone. It is relatively inexpensive to build app-like mobile websites that can be easily updated to support your business.

- Content still matters. Out-of-home boards need to be managed as carefully as the board creative itself. Marketers—large and small—can also add "mobile specials" for those who take the time to engage, such as a room or car upgrade, additional percentage off a meal, or added bonus with purchase.

- The ability to create a mobile relationship with a fan at a live venue is probably one of the greatest opportunities that exists for brands that sponsor.

- One of the best opportunities for activating outdoor and in-store experience is geotargeting and the data that gets unlocked at the most personal of levels. With consumer permission, we can ascertain much more information about who's buying, the type of phone they are using, the type of content they are engaging (demonstrating their interests for future experience development), and, of course, what's prompted them to buy either now or later.

- Social is the next obvious winner in geotargeting, allowing those who have just experienced a brand to instantly like it or report their poor experience. The company can immediately take appropriate action either way.

CHAPTER 10

Video Will Be Mobile's "Killer App"

Get Ready Now!

FOR A VERY BRIEF MOMENT, WE ARE GOING TO GO
all techno geek to demonstrate just how critical video will be
to mobile and to really anything we do in social, apps, and on
the entire web. This is a bold statement, but widespread video
is really starting to happen technologically and over the mobile
device in a very big way. It's subtle, as most technology waves
are, but video's impact will be evident very soon. If you just start
to look at your own phone and social apps on mobile, you'll see
how advanced video is becoming, as anyone can capture quality
video on their mobile device, edit it, and share it instantly to the
mobile networks, and do so at much faster transmission speeds.

The advances in mobile video communication we see from Facebook, Instagram, Twitter, Pinterest, and others are the leading edge of the technology wave. Increasingly, we are also seeing mobile personal communications advance quickly from voice to text to video. Facetime has become my favorite way to stay in touch with kids, other relatives, and close friends. My partner Mark and I constantly review video and TV projects from anywhere in the world through Facetime without having to download, send, and open multiple e-mails to do the same tasks. Facebook has allowed videos to auto-play in your newsfeed without audio until you click on it. This is an amazing marketing solution for both people and brands to get friends to engage with videos by starting to capture their attention with the motion and visual draw upon first glance of the thumbnails. It's also less intrusive to the consumer, as they don't have to hear videos unless they choose to. Viewers choosing to play a video is known in the industry as "intended view," and means that consumers have made a critical and conscious choice to watch a full video and audio from a brand or a person. Intended-view videos from brands are also among the highest value advertising units on digital platforms, especially mobile, since this is the primary platform consumers are engaged with socially and makes the sharing of videos as easy and natural as the impulse to do so.

Looking at it from the brands' perspective—which has long regarded video as the preferred form of communication with consumers because of the emotions, feelings, and messages that can be conveyed in just a few frames—brands are quickly shifting dollars to production and distribution of daily video content through all types of traditional and social channels. Our company is working with brands like Pedigree, Coca-Cola, and Budweiser that have an overwhelming desire to reach millions of their social followers—primarily through mobile—with daily, fresh video content. You don't have to look far to see how quickly video will alter the mobile and overall digital landscape.

DO YOU HEAR THAT? THE "MOBILE-VIDEO TSUNAMI" IS COMING!

Cisco, my favorite geeky company, annually releases its "Visual Networking Index (VNI) Global Mobile Data Traffic Forecast Update." The recently released findings and video growth projections, especially over mobile, are staggering. Let's put it this way: Cisco sums up 2012 as the year that global mobile data traffic grew 70 percent in just one year, which is nearly 12 times the growth size of the entire global Internet in 2000. For the data geeks, this amounts to global mobile data traffic of nearly 885 petabytes per month versus 75 petabytes per month over the Internet in 2000. Regardless of your math aptitude, this is unprecedented growth, especially from 2011 to 2012, let alone over the last decade or so. Of course, the mobile phone is demonstrating its impact on the world in general, and specifically on data transport.

You will be interested to note that mobile video traffic exceeded 50 percent of the total of all traffic for the first time in 2012, reaching a new peak of 51 percent. Of critical importance to brand owners and managers who are looking to deliver or activate video via mobile, mobile connection speeds more than doubled in 2012, helping ease concerns both about consumer engagement with video on mobile and the ability to quickly deliver it. Here are some stats from my friends at Cisco that highlight the massive global growth:

- For all mobile devices, the average mobile speeds in 2012 grew to 526 kilobits per second (kbps) from 248 kbps in the prior year. You don't have to know what that means exactly to see that average mobile speeds have nearly doubled.
- In 2012 smartphones saw average speeds of 2,064 kbps, up from 1,211 kbps in 2011.
- For tablets, since many are connected to WiFi networks, the average speed in 2012 was 3,683 kbps—a big leap from 2,030 kbps in 2011.

So, while Cisco highlights that only one-fifth of all mobile devices globally are smartphones, that number is expected to surge well above 50 percent by the end of 2017, and it likely won't be too long after that all phones will be considered smart. And looking ahead, here's why marketing teams and organizations should start readying their budgets to focus on mobile and video: The future is all about connectivity and video. And this future is not that far off. Take a look at a few of the stats of what's to come:

- Two-thirds of the world's mobile data traffic will be video by 2017. Mobile video will increase 16-fold between 2012 and 2017, accounting for over 66 percent of total mobile data traffic by the end of the forecast period.
- The average smartphone will generate 2.7 GB of traffic per month in 2017, an eight-fold increase over the 2012 average of 342 MB per month. Aggregate smartphone traffic in 2017 will be 19 times greater than it is today, with a Compounded Annual Growth Rate (CAGR) of 81 percent.
- By the end of 2013, the number of mobile-connected devices exceeded the number of people on earth, and by 2017 there will be nearly

1.4 mobile devices per capita. There will be over 10 billion mobile-connected devices in 2017.

- Mobile network connection speeds will increase seven-fold by 2017. The average mobile network connection speed (526 kbps in 2012) will exceed 3.9 megabits per second (Mbps) in 2017. The Middle East and Africa will have the strongest mobile data traffic growth of any region at 77 percent CAGR. This region will be followed by Asia Pacific at 76 percent and Latin America at 67 percent.

So in a nutshell, mobile data transportation will skyrocket. Video will dominate and be its jet fuel. Some of my tech friends tell me that this rate of speed will allow for video to travel to and from your phone faster than your current cable system can deliver to your TV. When I was in Japan a few years ago, they were already tweaking terrestrial broadcast TV (the old-fashioned way of delivering TV signals over the air) to phone and many Japanese commuters were enjoying streaming TV on their phones on trains, in their offices, or even in cars while driving. With data transport speeds increasing, we will definitely see a similar phenomenon of "everyday" video increasingly being consumed on smaller devices for longer periods of time.

And speaking of international markets, a large part of this growth will take place outside of English-speaking countries. On top of it all, the growth is taking place in a very compressed time frame, which means companies have to be very nimble with their business planning; something American companies in particular have not done since the crash of 2008.

Consider if someone presented an investment opportunity for any stock or business sector. Who wouldn't want to invest and innovate in businesses that will be benefited by a 16-fold increase in growth over the next 48 months, as mobile is expected to? There is little doubt that the world is going mobile and video will start to rival and surpass any other activity in terms of data. More importantly, people will start ditching texting as a primary form of mobile communication and simply record their thoughts on video for the world to see faster, easier, and more effectively than the written word.

David Sable, CEO of Y&R, says this: "The ability to produce quality video—from both a content and production perspective—is already fundamental to what we do. What is new and largely enhanced by mobile is the ability to distribute it to mass audiences very inexpensively and in a quality way—even on the smallest of screens. It creates a whole new level of consumer engagement that will both uplift the brand and drive sales."

THE WORLD IS ABOUT TO UNDERGO A "VIDEO RENAISSANCE" . . . ARE YOU READY?

When you see statistics like this, you have to realize that we are about to embark on yet another tech-driven renaissance. Renaissances are often defined as periods in history driven by technology innovations that connect people of common thoughts, beliefs, interests, or lifestyles, regardless of geography, resulting in social movements of grand scale. The current mobile renaissance is coming on the heels of the birth of the Internet in 1994 and social networks just a few years ago, some of the most important recent tech evolutions that have sparked multiple global social, cultural, and political movements—all in the last 20 or so years.

Now, according to the statistics, we are about to undergo a "Video Renaissance." Individuals are now armed with devices that contain capacities to record and edit videos that equals what massive movie and TV studios were able to do just a few decades ago. Billions of people will soon have the capability to produce, dream, and distribute video content at levels that boggle the mind, creating celebrities where traditional means proved long antiquated. Sure, YouTube has been a destination for every possible video, but even this platform is starting to feel the strain of way too much volume and is being usurped by social networks that make every individual a "destination," or dare I say his or her own TV channel. Even those who try to control creation and distribution will be like those attempting to thwart the spread of something as simple as the latest viral video or something as important as democracy in long-suppressed nations. In fact, we should reflect on the history of such renaissances and take clues to understand the sheer magnitude of the direction we're taking.

Video moving across mobile networks at the growth projections cited will not just create an explosion of channels and choices, but will make current video search mechanisms obsolete in a very short amount of time. Current media channels—already under threat—will see advertising dollars quickly move from medium and content in the macro environment to content produced by individual brands—from people to products—garnering micro-bursts of attention, eyeballs, and ratings, if these even exist after 2017. Brands with social and web pages tied to the written word and still images, traditional video channels, and online video marketplaces with complex search and viral engines will need to transform quickly or be made obsolete by new players and consumers alike.

Why is video going to explode? Think about your own habits. It's not just about the growth in speed and technical capability.

According to my friends at Facebook, 2013 was the year in the United States during which the mobile screen surpassed the TV screen for more minutes of view time. In fact, my good friend Carolyn Everson, who runs marketing solutions with brand partners at Facebook, tells me that the research shows people will look at their phones an average of more than 100 times a day. As she put it, "Looking at your phone is becoming more and more akin to blinking!" We are moving from common use to habitual use of the phones and as a result, we will see it encroach on other media habits.

MOBILE VIDEO CUTS THROUGH
LANGUAGE AND LITERACY BARRIERS

With this kind of use of video over mobile, more times than not, video will increasingly help tell stories, in just a few seconds or minutes, that would take thousands of words and thousands of minutes to consume, especially on mobile devices. Don't get me wrong, I love a great book, and great authors, performers, and news people create words worth reading. But when it comes to everyday messages from friends or how-to information, nothing beats watching video. It's more about time savings in consuming everyday content and also about effectiveness in getting the most out of life. Recently, I was putting together a bike and I thought it would be so much easier if I could see a video of someone assembling it rather than trying to figure out part AA from part LL. This is why channels devoted entirely to cooking, fitness, and home improvement have become so popular. Yet, unlike broadcast quality TV, consumers will have much lower expectations to get things done faster. I don't need an Academy Award–winning cameraman to capture and deliver a video on bike assembly, I just need it to be clear, accurate, and presentable on a mobile phone.

My partner Mark Berryhill, who is co-founder of our company Unconventional Partners and now produces a number of TV shows and specials, as well as being a branded content pioneer as co-creator of Video Solutions for Meredith, a company that reaches 100 million women a month, knows this firsthand. "Brands from Kraft to the Home Depot, J&J, and more came to us not just because they wanted to reach millions and millions of women with more effective branded video content, but because they wanted the content for their everyday needs across a number of their owned platforms, such as in-store, web, and now, mobile. The everyday content needs from brands for fresh, relevant videos will only grow in the mobile era."

Another consideration for video becoming the primary mode of communication is the barriers to other forms of communication—largely the written word—we still see today that will not ease anytime soon. There is a large segment of the world's brand-consuming population that is largely illiterate, so reading of any language is not possible. In addition, many can't speak or write English even though many English-language brands still largely communicate in this language. Beyond language, there are multiple cultural barriers that make the written word largely evasive, or even offensive.

Video is a communication tool that breaks through the literacy barriers, dialects, and markets in ways already imagined for TV. While we have to be cognizant of cultural considerations when producing content, video, music, and images are so vital to any marketing campaign and will become increasingly so in the mobile age. Plus, we will start to see apps and other tools emerge that instantly translate video to one's own language, or even dialect, in the blink of an eye. This will transform communication between cultures, business units, and political bodies. From the individual to the corporation, video will start to replace text e-mails, text messages, and text instructions.

THERE'S A REASON MOBILE SCREENS RESEMBLE TV SCREENS

With so much video being increasingly delivered over mobile, we will start to demand and see improvement in its quality. The mobile screen was crafted very much in the vein of the original TV screen. Its pixelation and vibrant colors make high-definition video as enjoyable as that viewed on larger screens. I have found that the only way for me to catch up with some of the most popular TV series is on my mobile device. As such, video for everyday consumption is more easily accepted on mobile as TV devices. Do I think a 50-inch TV screen is better than a mobile screen for most entertainment, sports, and long-form video viewing? Of course I do. Do I think the mobile screen is more practical for our constantly moving lives? Absolutely. Am I willing to sacrifice quality of viewing for the ability to view anywhere? Yes, for most forms of video entertainment and certainly all forms of everyday communications from brands and with my friends, co-workers, and others.

I, like many of you, am finding myself constantly streaming live video to my mobile. When it comes to life's essential content—traffic, weather, news—I actually prefer the mobile device, and it requires no reason to be on a larger screen. Live streaming of video on mobile has long been commonplace in places like Brazil, Japan, and Germany. Live mobile viewing is a way of life and is much more advanced than in the United States. It's here I learned that many channels actually have two sub-channels. One is the actual live channel. The other has tune-in content on a continual, repeating loop that gives the rushed, commuting mobile viewer a taste, but also the ability to click through to the main channel for longer-form content if they have the time, interest, and signal strength.

The future plans of phone makers show focus on the screen and camera, especially video and sound functions. It's clear that improvements to the technology of mobile devices will center on advancing the experience for video and audio capture and delivery with less focus on the written interface. We are also seeing the diffusion of technologies and skills—that were once very advanced—to produce, edit, and distribute TV-quality video. I met an artist who only called herself Sonja at a SoHo art gallery who told me she was working on an art installation of videos captured exclusively on her iPhone. Just like we do in our production studios, she manipulated some of the video images on a computer application and added on-screen graphics. In just a few minutes, she had video product that was indistinguishable from professional videos. She is not alone. Many of us are capturing history—both personal and of the world around us—on video. Such diffused video capability and technical ability to distribute will make all of us like Sonja, whether just to our Facebook and Tumblr communities or to a large, commercial audience like Sonja is hoping to capture in one of the art centers of the world.

MOBILE HASTENS ADVERTISERS AS MEDIA PLATFORMS

Major consumer brands—both media and hard goods—have the greatest opportunity to leverage the amazing reach—earned, owned, paid—to build new video channels to market, starting with creating much more of their own video content, content from other brands (media), procuring the soon-to-be-viral assets from their masses of consumers and fans, among other sources. Some brands are dipping their toes in the proverbial pool by cultivating ideas for TV spots and other branded content from social networks, their media partners, and most ardent, loyal customers. One compelling example is what Frito-Lay did to harvest ideas from its brand loyalists for its Super Bowl advertising through the web and social networks while using its packaging to promote the opportunity. Consumers were given a brand brief just like the advertising agencies and told to create a 30-second TV spot on their own. One winner would have their entry appear in the Super Bowl. The initial campaign was so successful that it led to more such initiatives from Frito-Lay and now, a number of other brands have jumped on board to cultivate creative ideas from their most ardent fans. It probably scared the professional advertising creative community because the spots were procured so inexpensively, and my understanding is that many created, edited, and submitted their entries with a mobile device.

While this is a great example of success, many other brands are warned not to do this because of the severe risk of unintended consequences—especially with a brand identity. Advertising professionals advise that leaving your brand exposed to the masses for creative input will both surface good ideas for the brand as well as many negative ones. These consumer-as-creative-director activities, though, are still a blip on the marketing radar. However, what it demonstrates is that mobile video capabilities are in the hands of everyone who has a smartphone. There is little doubt that consumers will adopt video as a primary form of communication, transcending borders, barriers, languages, and consumer groups.

Websites largely have not changed since being unveiled in 1994. Sure, we have added video players and enlarged—dare I say, engorged—the size of ads, but very little has been done to prepare for a mostly video and mobile future. I hope this is a wake-up call for brands to recognize that they will not just need to have more video-based content to compete, they will also need to produce it in languages other than English. My call to action is simple. Start the video conversion process now as a global or company-wide strategy along with mobile delivery as the primary means of distribution. By starting to add mobile delivery of video, brands can plan properly and dub for language and culture in the near term, and for the longer term they can consider how to develop content efficiently and effectively for worldwide use. Distribution will largely and increasingly occur on mobile, especially as smarter and smaller devices are introduced in the next few years. Now is the time to start assessing all of your marketing and communications and pinpointing those that can be converted to video.

EMBARKING ON YOUR BRAND'S VIDEO PLANS

Given the growing trend toward video, where do brands begin?

Find Your Video Voice

First you need to find your "video voice." Similar to brand strategy and creative planning, many companies typically have resources in their creative or other agencies who are helping produce 30-second TV spots or other video-based content. This is a great place to begin on what kind of voice, talent, graphics, and other elements you can include in videos that are posted on the web, social, or delivered with mobile activation of traditional and digital media. Companies may be able to tap existing endorsements or bring in talent specifically to produce the necessary content going forward. Remember that the basics of the video need to be the basics of mobile marketing; this means that you must be customer-centric, fitting into a strategy that complements other areas of marketing without recycling TV ads or other media created for other outlets and purposes.

Start Small, but Start Something

Next, you want to start by taking small video steps. Some companies attempt video with little understanding of how to do it, a lack of research into what consumers will react favorably to, or they are tempted to jump in the video "pool" with both feet, seeking to convert all content at once. But this can place too much pressure on the organization, and nothing gets accomplished as a result. It's best to start prudently and cautiously with a few videos to support an upcoming advertising campaign or with evergreen online content that will return on the investment over a long period.

Mark Berryhill says this about co-founding Meredith Video Solutions: "We began our video solutions unit and the company continues production today around very 'pedestrian' video content for brands to use on web and social sites. Kraft, for example, had us produce recipe videos for their website in eight different languages with eight different sets of talent. The videos allow them to be helpful to families and appeal to them in the cultural tone of their varied target audiences at very inexpensive costs."

Starting with a smaller number of videos allows the company to test voice and adjust easily, understand its processes to accomplish, and then, with some small successes, to set forth a system to expand the production, the reach, and the performance of converting communications and marketing to video.

I met with a well-known business-to-business brand that also markets heavily in the consumer space given size and importance of the small to midsize business sector. We met with several executives who were looking to build a mobile experience with their TV spots during a popular sporting event. Their digital team did not really understand how to use video content for a mobile experience. So they sent customers to a very dense, wordy site containing a white paper (over 7,000 words) that was the subject being promoted in the ads.

I realize this was a first attempt at a mobile campaign, but what they could have done was produce a video and consider a series of online or live seminars on the subject in key cities. The videos could either be produced in a timely fashion and dubbed for multiple languages or produced in such a way that multiple languages could be generated later while still keeping the production to one day. We suggested doing a 90-second main video describing the benefits of the company's solutions with additional 30- to 60-second discrete video segments delving deeper into specific subject matter. They could certainly accompany the videos with the full white paper, but our goal was to engage prospects from the get-go with a menu of solution options that would take very little time to consume, yet prompt the prospect to indicate sales interest or be receptive when a salesperson from the company would call.

Everyday Video Can Be Everyday in Quality

Whether your company is large or small, the content of your video does not need to be high gloss or Academy Award quality to be effective. I work with a number of creative advertising agencies who have built budgets, careers, and industry awards by producing just 30 seconds of TV ads with budgets that barely drop below $500,000. This cost, production, or creative model is not sustainable as we embark into what I term "everyday video."

Everyday video is virtually every video that will not appear on TV. If you buy into the notion that most video will be consumed from mobile activation of scan codes as well as on websites and social pages, the quality can cover a wide range and still be effective. Zappos is a very good example of a company that is beginning to incorporate video into its buying experience, because nothing can quite convey the look and feel of clothes, shoes, and accessories like video. As retail discovers the opportunity to sell with video, we are going to also have to find cost-effective ways to do it.

Walmart is another example of a brand that produces a significant amount of local video with an agency called Vimby (Video in My Backyard, a Mark Burnett and Hearst company). This company has high-quality producers all over the country who produce weekly local spots for dozens of Walmart's key TV markets. This allows Walmart to be nimble given local market conditions, events, weather, and price matching among competitors. I don't think it will be long before this video component expands to provide fresh, daily content for Walmart's web, social, and in-store purposes.

Cost and Quality Can Be Mutually Exclusive—Be Leery of Budget-Breaking Budgets

"Branded content" is another one of those misnomers right up there with "mobile optimized." Branded content is typically video content that is fully or co-produced with the brand's product, positioning, messages, target audiences, locations or talent integrated throughout and leads to a favorable response by consumers including sharing to the point that it's "viral" or well-saturated in the market. Not all branded content needs are the same, and in many cases the brand brief is completely ignored by media producers who are more concerned about expressing their own creativity than achieving the brand's objectives. In these early days of branded video content and programming, we have seen mixed results as exorbitant budgets and creative ideas become the focus while brands are relegated to afterthought status. Brands often make the mistake that longer-form video or high-production quality is critical to mobile. The fact is that most consumers watch big videos on big screens. You want a snack-sized viewing experience on mobile. Sure, longer form videos can be served over mobile, but when it comes to branded content versus highly produced entertainment, the attention branded content is given will shrink with the struggle it may take to watch continually on a smaller screen. If consumers want more or longer-form branded content, offer them more. My suggestion is that mobile videos need to range from a few seconds to no more than a few minutes. One example is a major consumer product (CPG) brand that created a 15-minute video for a big awards show. No one watched more than a few seconds of the video, and it actually had significant abandon rates as soon as the length of the video loaded and was visible to the viewer.

If you are a smaller company such as a restaurant or retail outlet, you may want to think about how video can help sell your business. In the case of a restaurant, you may want to show your fabulous ambiance, amazing food, or delightful private events. To start on these low-production ventures, I always suggest to friends and family to contact a local university with a good broadcast or video media program. Talk to the dean's office to see if you can hire a student to produce the video. It's often a great learning experience for students to put on their résumés, cost effective, and often of passable and, in many cases, of higher quality than expected for the business owner.

David Sable says this about mobile and local businesses of all sizes: "Brands need to understand if I'm on my smartphone,

I'm ready to look to buy. We need to understand their motiva-
tion and give them tools that are not only efficient but create
an engaging user experience. That's why video on mobile packs
such power."

A friend of mine once owned several pizza shops and for just
a few hundred dollars, he hired a local student to do a series of
four 45-second videos on different aspects of his business, rang-
ing from the great food to the great atmosphere for watching
sports. He met with a college senior who was majoring in mass
media. They discussed the approach, exchanged ideas, educated
each other on their respective crafts, and settled on a "storyboard"
sketched out on a napkin. Once completed, the business owner
had a whole new selling proposition conveyed with short videos
for his website and the scan codes for his exterior menu board.
Bookings, especially for the highly profitable catering and parties, began to rise thanks to an inexpensive yet effective way to
promote his business. Branded content can be very utilitarian in
nature and often is pretty "pedestrian" because we need to attract
sales from—you guessed it—pedestrians.

Large brands can get creative in sourcing video that could
even be free and come from your most ardent fans. Many big
brands live and die by brand briefs for a product. I never quite
understood the brand brief, but in short, it's a one-pager for a
short-term campaign with the brand's key product focus, audiences, related messages, and key selling points. It serves as the
basis for generating creative ideas before one or more are selected
for execution. Most brand briefs are used to create 30-second
TV spots or other forms of advertising, yet they can also be used
as a way to source and filter videos from employees, customers,

and social fans. Ardent brand lovers on social networks can sometimes be the best sources of videos, and while the shelf-life may be limited, use and rights can be very easy and inexpensive to obtain. In some cases, you can just ask for rights in exchange for the notoriety and social fame. Others may be satisfied with some minor monetary or gift card compensation. In any case, the social and customer base will increasingly be populated by people who are adept at video production and telling a brand story from the heart. In my humble opinion, nothing sways a new customer like authentic brand love from a loyal customer, whether conveyed as a handwritten letter to the CEO all the way up to a video that goes viral across social networks.

Source Video from your Media Partners

Look for "video creation moments" that are available to you in your current marketing situation or happening around you every day. Many brands are actually buying integrations in TV shows, sponsorships or other forms of media with a major buying commitment. Obviously, these media partners have the capability to produce videos or other content for everyday use that may not appear in the show, brand integration, or overall media buy. If you have not discussed expanded video production needs with your media partners, it's something you can explore as a value-add to your media buys. It gives you the awareness from the buy, but then produces marketing assets you can use on your own web and social sites, among other places.

Our own daily TV property, *OK! TV*, which is a good-natured entertainment news show based on the global celebrity magazine, is increasingly producing segments for such brands as Pedigree, Coca-Cola, Budweiser, and Panera Bread, among others. Sure, these brands are interested in the reach *OK! TV* has nationally, but they are equally and sometimes more interested in having fresh video content for their web, social, and other owned distribution points.

The link is natural. Many media companies that are selling brands on their advertising inventory and show integration opportunities are also beginning to move into custom production, largely stemming from the existing buys brands are already doing. Increasingly, we are seeing TV producers becoming more adept at naturally and organically integrating brands into content. This can be a simple, yet effective and efficient way to start building a company's video assets.

However, media companies who are increasing revenue and skills in producing video for TV or digital buys are often not allowing the brands to use the video for web or social pages. Always negotiate hard for open use of content produced by a media partner, which is paid for by your brand. Lawyers will also intervene and claim that rights use is limited, especially with talent. I don't buy it. My response is, get your media partner to provide solutions that are not limited by rights, use, or imagination. If you are paying for it, it shouldn't only run on the media partner's show and platforms. Brands should be allowed to use video across their mobile, social, or other platforms. Trust me, this will not be easy. The larger the media platform, the more it will fight brands to keep a tight lid on the video content. But many are learning the value of allowing the brands to use the integrated content on their own social, web, and mobile pages because of the obvious awareness building it does for the media brand, at minimum, to building a longer term relationship with advertising brands.

Many media partners actually are more than happy to either add or *pro bono* additional content outside of the use for the intended media plan. More and more agencies are working on behalf of clients to clear rights so brands can either take content from the programs or use additional content produced for their web and social sites.

Our TV show, *OK! TV*, is a half-hour daily entertainment show airing in most of the United States. It's very celebrity and brand friendly and lends itself to lifestyle video segments and content that brands can use after airing on any platform they choose. For Jamba Juice, we created some video segments with its celebrity franchisee and spokesperson, Venus Williams, that the company can now use in stores, on the web, or via mobile, activated from free-standing inserts in newspapers or window decals on store fronts.

Actress Kate Hudson started an inexpensive, high-quality workout clothing line, and she came to *OK! TV* to produce segments with her co-developer of the workout clothes, who also happened to be her Pilates and fitness instructor. Given that Kate's business partner was also a fitness expert, we produced video segments that highlighted exercise routines featuring the functionality and fashionable nature of the workout clothes. Kate's company then used the segment for both her web and trade sales efforts to stores that were considering distributing her clothes, giving the brand a boost in both consumer awareness and sales tools for building her business with the retail trade.

With both brands, Jamba Juice and Kate Hudson combined their media buys with the need for everyday video, creating a highly effective, cost-efficient, and well-produced series for all of their marketing needs, especially the ones that will be activated by mobile.

Mobile speeds, technologies, and viewing screens are going to vastly improve and accelerate video delivery. Buzzfeed is a prime example of a site that is quickly transforming the world of branded content. Brands are increasingly tapping Buzzfeed's producers with their brand messages to create branded video content integral to the launch of entire marketing campaigns. Buzzfeed produces for, targets, distributes to, and clearly communicates to the viewer or reader that it has engaging branded content. They are proving that marketing and online communications will quickly transform from the written word to video communications reaching and touching anyone in the world. For every person in the world will not only be armed with a smartphone in the very near future, but they will also likely have more than one device, and video creation and consumption will be a primary activity. Now is the time to get your own company to start thinking, creating, and building effective and cost-efficient ways to produce videos to sell your businesses and ideas.

CHAPTER 10: THUMB'S UP TIPS

- According to Cisco, the mobile platform is advancing so quickly, video is poised to be the primary form of communication and marketing in a very short amount of time.
  - Two-thirds of the world's mobile data traffic will be video by 2017.
  - At the end of 2013, the number of mobile-connected devices exceeded the number of people on earth, and by 2017 there will be nearly 1.4 mobile devices per capita.
  - Mobile network connection speeds will increase seven-fold by 2017.
- Find your video voice by considering what kind of content, talent, graphics, and other elements should be included in videos that are posted on your web or social sites, or that are delivered with mobile activation of traditional and digital media.
- Start down the video path by starting small. Start by creating just a few videos that can live on your web and social sites and expand plans from there.
- Videos do not have to be six-figure budget breakers, but rather can be done by inexpensive local videographers, students majoring in broadcast, or media partners looking to get your media buy with video as a bonus.
- Source your video production needs from current partners like social fans, loyal customers, and media partners who have the capability to build awareness with a traditional media buy, but can also give you the video content for use on your sites or produce video content just for this purpose.

CHAPTER 11

Data Gatherers

The More You Give, the More You Get

THE POWER OF MOBILE DATA . . . AND THE THREAT

You can hardly have a book about emerging forms of mobile marketing without talking about data. Like many brand and business owners, I have always had a mixed relationship with data because while being amazed at the kind of data increasingly captured in the mobile and digital world, I am equally troubled as an average citizen about what is known about me and how it may be used or even abused. To understand this point, you don't have to look much further than the Google financial settlement with a number of U.S. states over tracking online consumers without the consumer's knowledge. My simple rule as a marketer has always been, "Do unto others as you wish done to you."

Increasingly and especially with mobile devices, the ability and temptation to capture data without the consumer's knowledge has never been easier. Sophisticated brands that have long and storied capabilities to derive sound marketing strategies are well ahead of the rest of the world when it comes to advanced use of data to get messages to the people most likely to buy. Many emerging mobile businesses from the tech centers of Silicon Valley, Israel, Brazil, and Ireland, among others, are being founded on the extensive "data exhaust" being put out by mobile phones.

George Kliavkoff, who runs Hearst's Ventures arm and is co-president of the company's Entertainment and Syndication Group, had this insightful comment: "Data exhaust creates businesses that could have never existed before and is connected to the mobile network."

Data exhaust is simply the data on location, content viewing, and other elements naturally emitted by phones. The main issue quickly arising for marketers is determining what data they can voluntarily "sniff" and what data is proprietary to the user. This debate will likely rage further, especially as technology allows for complete detection of your life as experienced through the mobile phone. Not to get all political on everyone, but it's quite possible that in the United States and in other democracies, we will see amendments to constitutions and laws emerging to protect citizens as well as to provide robust abilities for brands to gather and use data. However, this is a discussion for a different book. For now, marketers should be aware of privacy laws and keep a close eye on developments that may affect marketing campaigns and most importantly perception of brands that are thought by consumers to cross the line.

Kliavkoff highlights that there are always start-ups that take advantage of such niche developments as data exhaust, but there are also some established players in very traditional media. He highlights some surprising statistics about sports juggernaut ESPN: "ESPN has embraced mobile for everything, and toward the end of 2013 they realized that 50 percent of their traffic is now mobile usurping the desktop screens. On a time-spent basis, more of their consumption happens on mobile. The lines have now crossed." Clearly, ESPN realizes the benefit of delivering content on sport fans' favorite teams to any screen even though the primary form of revenue has come from TV. However, with the majority of viewers now engaging on mobile, ESPN can also realize new, high-value revenue with data-infused mobile advertising inventory.

Kliavkoff also brings Buzzfeed to our attention regarding growing mobile revenue: "One of the issues with mobile is the CPMs and the advertising inventory has, up to now, been relatively low (relative to other screens). Buzzfeed doesn't sell buttons or banners. [Buzzfeed] stumbled into the idea that if it's native advertising through sponsored stories, you get paid the same exact number of dollars as you would if it's viewed on mobile as you do on desktop. It is the first generation content company that doesn't suffer from the move to mobile from other platforms (and the loss of display ads and revenue)."

Because Buzzfeed delivers new content recommendations based on the data of your past content consumption, it actually has benefited from the consumer's shift to mobile. While other media companies are encumbered by differing between the screens, type of ads, and pricing, start-ups like Buzzfeed are selling sponsored content with advertisers only paying on views of the content, regardless of the screen type. The advertiser has paid for the story to be read or the video to be watched whether TV, desktop, or mobile. The consumer wins because, similar to Amazon and Netflix, Buzzfeed is using far richer mobile data—that in many ways is voluntary because content interests are natural—to deliver more relevant content to users, which moves more consumers to engage and creates more value for advertisers. So brands can be sure that a sponsored, yet expertly developed story, will reach an audience ready to engage because their interest in the subject is high. A brand's own social networks are another place to leverage such content. Followers are loyalists.

VOLUNTARY DATA IS STILL ALWAYS MORE VALUABLE THAN INVOLUNTARY DATA

It's important to delineate between what I term "voluntary" versus "involuntary" data. Voluntary data is the data that consumers allow or give up to a brand, which could be anything from clothing size, food taste preferences, address, and more. Involuntary data is what can be increasingly detected without consumers knowing, such as exact location, how much time is spent in an aisle of a grocery store, or the average time spent on a mobile device per month. Of course, there are other examples, but my point is that brands find it much easier to get the involuntary data and still be able to create marketing strategies that are cost effective and much cleaner than those involving the consumer directly. That said, voluntary data is actually much richer, more complex, largely accurate, and can help refine personalized marketing messages that are increasingly possible with the personal devices of phones. However, involving the consumer through voluntary data is often messy, inconsistent, and prone to cause suspicion among the target audience.

Carol Kruse, one of the best-known marketers with stints as chief of marketing at ESPN and chief digital marketer at Coca-Cola, says this: "Mobile and loyalty programs are ones that we leveraged at live events. When we sponsored events, participants were encouraged to go through our brand's loyalty program on the mobile phone for the chance to win instant upgrades in seats, meet the performer backstage, and more. It delivered a wealth of entertainment to the loyalists and data back to the brand."

The good news for brands is that we can increasingly deliver benefits to consumers who provide voluntary data and agree to allow brands to sniff their involuntary data through the mobile device. Businesses such as Waze—a GPS mapping system—and Shazam now use a combination of data points to help customers get to their destinations faster or get more of the content they love. Waze is the first generation smart GPS mapping system that tracks users' phone exhaust to help others following them to find the fastest routes from point A to point B. Waze also will detect certain times of the day when the app is engaged, such as asking if you want to be directed home at the end of a work day, which both minimizes the time needed by the user to input the address, but will likely trigger different types of ads that appear on the user's screen when the car is not in motion (which is also detected by the app). Then, at stop lights, Waze will deliver a coupon offer for a to-go order at a restaurant on the route home. Its worth to everyone in the value chain is immense and all win. Consumers gladly give up their mobile phone exhaust and data for faster routes all the time, guaranteed. Ads tailored to my interests or routes are, frankly, a welcome bonus to ads that are just run-of-site or random. Others such as Netflix, Amazon, and Google—which purchased Waze—are jumping on to the value exchange bandwagon, increasingly seek to deliver a customer benefit in tandem with building rich voluntary and involuntary data profiles on users. The value exchange is clear to the consumer and the value of the data received is limitless.

George Kliavkoff, has this advice for media companies seeking to get more from consumers: "You have to start by being purpose driven. You have to give someone a reason to check their phone, whether delivering the weather or helping them be five minutes earlier in their commute." Clearly, the value can be subtle, but the returned interaction and data from the consumer can be invaluable.

Another example of the power of voluntary data captured on mobile devices can be highlighted in a chapter of my early entrepreneurial life—which was not all that long ago—when I spent an idealistic 18 months both investing in and working with a company that was founded on the simple premise that if consumers voluntarily give up data about themselves, we can deliver ads and brand messages of the most relevance. While it initially failed as a business concept, it reflected my entire point of view on data in the digital and mobile age: that the more you give in terms of benefit to consumers, the more they will willingly give up data about themselves and allow ongoing data collection even without their full knowledge. Regardless of my own business success or failure on this front, the "more you do, the more you get" philosophy is evident in such new mobile first movers as Waze, Shazam, and Netflix. In addition, we also have to be very cautious in our pursuit and leverage of data; just because you can technically do it doesn't mean it's ethical. Common sense and common courtesy typically define ethics. Again, with each circumstance the age-old question arises: "Would I want this done to me?"

During my interview with George Kliavkoff, my mobile phone rang. In a feature from Apple, the phone provided a prompt to decline the call with a question to "Remind Me" when you move a certain distance from where the call was received. George explained: "This is known as drawing a 'geo-fence' and using your entrance and exit from this geo-fence to initiate an action. The function is one of many examples you can create from sensors." Yet it's another example of giving up data for a benefit in return and in this case, it's a highly personal "geo-fence."

My philosophy about data is simple, whether it's my location or a list of my travels across the web. All data is the intellectual property of the user. Period. However, many platforms and brands—especially in mobile—don't share this philosophy. Many think that use of their platform is value enough to the consumer in exchange for their data. This may be true in many instances. In yet other instances, some platforms are pretty seductive in what they garner and how they use it, often without the full knowledge of or benefit to the consumer. A primary example of this is when you join a site's membership program, visit a site for the first time, or make an online purchase; most will prompt with a now perfunctory check-off stating that you understand the terms and conditions of use. Sure, every site, including ones I run in the media space, has terms and conditions that cover both data capture and use. However, few of us have ever actually read these terms, and even fewer of us fully understand what is being captured or how it's being used. In fact, I have now turned my AOL account into my de facto e-mail account for all commercial and brand purposes. This way I keep my other e-mails pristine of junk and unwanted offers. It has worked. My AOL inbox reaches 150 or more e-mails a day, many of which are from brands that acquired my data probably several times over to market anti-balding, anti-aging, and anti-fat solutions to me. In addition to not feeling very good about myself when I see my inbox, I am also stymied by the hundreds of messages a week that flow to my AOL account from years of giving up my e-mail with little or no knowledge of how it's being exploited. The question it begs is, as the virtual world proliferates and expands via mobile, where does such use of data and intrusion end without self- or government-imposed regulation on companies?

IT'S ABOUT MORE THAN CONSUMER PROTECTION, IT'S ABOUT TRUST AND VALUE

To further expand on this notion of data and use, it really comes down to two simple principles: does the consumer trust the platform, and do they see value in the exchange of their property for the experience? A few years ago, when former senator John Kerry (D-MA) and senator John McCain (R-AZ) proposed a bipartisan bill to protect the data privacy rights of citizens, they were met with staunch resistance by the advertising industry.

In an effort to thwart the bill going forward, leaders from the advertising and media sectors met with lawmakers from both parties. They told the lawmakers that if they curtailed gathering and use of consumer data, it would render their own campaign advertising efforts so inefficient that both parties would have to double their already lofty budgets of roughly $1 billion each for their nominated candidate's presidential election efforts. Let's just say that the death of the Kerry/McCain bill was very swift.

As technology continues to evolve, the ability to tap one's data will only increase, and with it will come ethical, legal, and moral questions on what can be shared with whom. One prediction gaining credence is that we will one day soon have an Amendment to the Constitution outlining the rights for all on the data front. This may sound trite, but companies in the mobile space who give as much, if not more, value in return will see consumers giving up more data and doing so very willingly.

Waze is an application developed in Israel that was bought by Google for approximately $1 billion. This app is a driver's best friend because of the way it detects phone data from drivers along a route. It uses data exhaust to detect the best and fastest ways to drive from point A to point B, thus the brand name Waze. It is stunning how this has gone beyond GPS technology of static maps to one that tracks a driver's location, speed, upcoming hazards, and redirects to even the most uncommon or unheard-of routes. While the potential uses of this technology—such as detecting when I am speeding—conjure up images of *Minority Report*, I know that most times I don't break the law and therefore take my risks to get to the fastest routes possible.

As a consumer, I marvel at the precision of data capture to our second-by-second, millimeter-by-millimeter movements and our own willingness to give up significant involuntary (where we are) and voluntary (where we are going) information to have our quality of life instantly improved. I can tell you firsthand that I'll happily receive any advertising delivered in a safe manner because it's relevant to my location, time of day, or interests based on past travels, social posts, and other data to which I have granted brands permission to access. The value to me as a marketer is beyond obvious on every level—information, delivery, engagement, and purchase.

George Kliavkoff continues: "The phones we all carry now have a dozen and soon to be a couple of dozen sensors built into them. Each of these sensors throw off data exhaust that for the first time ever is available, shareable, and connectable to virtual networks. Uber [a mobile car and taxi service] is another example, [as it connects] a driver that has excess capacity to a passenger who happens to be around the corner. This way it connects the buyers and sellers of a service [much more quickly] only because they are sharing their locations over a common network."

Most recently, I have noticed that Waze will deliver pop-up ads when I am stopped at a red light or gas station. These are often relevant ads to my surroundings. By tapping the ad, I can engage right then and there or save for later. Over time, the ads will become even more targeted based on location, time of day, and past GPS-tracked retailer locations. To me, this is the perfect nexus of providing a value of direct relevance in return for my most trusted personal data—my whereabouts. Consumers will be much more receptive to the advertising messages because having this app for free makes ads, as well as the data they have now captured, much more tolerable.

Kliavkoff points out something else: "I am not even sure that revenue is the Google play [with such acquisitions as Waze]. They are looking at the rich data now captured for helping to make everyday searches more meaningful and improve their other map products along with it." Advertising could be of interest as a revenue source, but I tend to agree that initially, Google is looking to catapult ahead with mobile-generated data that complements its search, mail, maps, YouTube, and other platforms and applications.

David Sable says this: "A majority of searches on phone are to buy something. A majority of these searches come with the expectation of buying something within a few blocks. This is where local businesses can seal the deal with a real value exchange."

Facebook has recently introduced an ad product that detects key words and phrases in user posts and delivers ads to those people in the News Feed. Remember, more than 550 million people access Facebook each day through mobile. Carolyn Everson, the executive at Facebook who runs global marketing solutions for brand partners, tells me: "Consumers share data with us every day by simply creating for and going to the News Feed feature. This is where we are now putting a majority of our sponsored messages and target based on what key words people are creating or stopping to read. The more people use Facebook, the better the experience and more relevant the advertising messages. The ability to effectively target on mobile is better than the 'Holy Grail' of all other forms of targeted mobile advertising because we have seen our revenue from sponsored and targeted News Feed entries go from zero to nearly half of revenue in just about 18 months."

That said, there is very little doubt that tapping the individual posts of users and delivering messages of direct relevance will be readily accepted by the consumer, even if this practice falls in the category of using involuntary data. This strategy is exactly what I was hoping to accomplish in my failed attempt to match brands to consumers most likely to buy.

Just this morning, I saw the benefit firsthand. This year, my alma mater—Florida State University—won the BCS National Championship in football. Of course I, like the legion of many other fans, have been rabidly posting on my Facebook page. Within a few days of finding out that FSU would play in the big game, I began receiving ads for championship gear, tickets, travel, and more. There is little doubt that the messages are on target and aimed at my own words, interests, lifestyles, and hobbies. There is clearly a value exchange that allows me to embrace these ads on Facebook instead of merely tolerating them, because they are now directly relevant to me.

Carol Kruse, world-renowned marketer, encourages giving relevance and purpose: "Mobile marketing has to enhance the consumer experience, not disrupt it. The personal nature of the device makes it a very fine line. We need to take the data we have to deliver an experience that is relevant, gives purpose to the consumer, and, as a result, is effective."

Hulu, a streaming TV service, is another company that is also beginning to use content consumption and purchase behavior to not just deliver targeted messages for movies, but to also deliver the brands that share the attributes and/or target audiences of content choices—be it TV, movie or print. By being the one of the largest "content on demand" providers, there is little doubt that Hulu understands the content habits of many of its users.

Rich Riley, CEO of Shazam, sums it up best: "We have more than 500 million Shazams each month [2013]. People held out their arm, pressed a button on their phone, and there was nothing subtle about their actions. They really want to know what that content is. So, we have people amassing in the millions around interests in music, TV, and taking those preferences and data to target the most relevant market to them. So, if someone likes Bruno Mars, who better than Shazam to notify them of the new song, or if you are Pepsi and want to get closer to those interested in Bruno Mars, then we can help identify the 20 million plus people who engaged Shazam around him when hearing his music and/or watching his appearances on TV."

GAINING DATA, INSIGHTS, SALES, AND RELATIONSHIPS—THE KEYS TO SUCCESS

Data value exchange is an increasingly compelling proposition for both businesspeople and their customers, especially over mobile. How can you join the value exchange, whether you are a small dry cleaning business or a huge multinational with very sophisticated data collection methods?

PERMISSION IS THE KEY TO GETTING CONSUMERS TO GIVE UP DATA

What Shazam, Waze, and Facebook have in common—along with Netflix, Amazon, and others—with such rich data is that they are indirectly asking for permission to deliver brand messages of direct relevance. They have hit on what I think is the most fundamental principle in securing and using consumer data today: permission.

Permission can come in many forms. It goes beyond the obligatory "Terms and Conditions" that all companies employ to detail their privacy and data capture/use policies, which many of us blindly check off. However, when I think of permission, I think of conscientious attempts by brands to engage consumers to actively allow their data to be captured and leveraged in ways that are clear and intended (instead of the practice of some dubious players using data in unintended ways, such as selling it to other brands).

I was recently in a high-end retail store when the sales clerk presented me with a beautiful embossed card to fill out. When I inquired as to the benefit of filling out the card, I was told it was for marketing purposes. "That's it?" I thought. "There are no special preview nights for new collections they would invite me to? There are no special sales or offers for giving up my information, especially when they have excess merchandise in my size?

There's no free gift in return or extra percentage off for giving up my very valuable information?" I slid the card back over the beautifully ornate sales counter and told the sales associate, "No, thank you."

When I left the corporate world to become an investor and entrepreneur, I got involved with a now defunct business and concept called AdGenesis. It was a simple premise where consumers would join and give up information about their lifestyles, interests, and upcoming purchase intentions, and in a value exchange, they would be matched with brands of direct relevance. Furthermore, the consumer would be rewarded for paying attention to brand messages. Think of it as the Match.com of consumers and brands. It was brilliant—at least I thought it was—and much needed in a world where advertising was growing by platform, especially mobile.

In the early days of brand matching, consumers loved it. They were welcoming to brand messages of all types because the service we were creating asked them about their upcoming purchase intentions such as a new car, TV, or outfit for Saturday night. I could get messages and offers that would engage. In fact, we had significant brand engagement, but this proved too cumbersome for advertisers who were used to the digital cleanness of sniffing data, and asking or involving the consumer directly was messy in comparison. Also, the whole incentive feature we created to reward consumers and prove that they paid attention was absolutely a no-no for advertisers who didn't believe in rewarding viewers for paying attention to their messages. In hindsight, we probably should have separated the matching versus reward features. Regardless, it led, as most failed concepts do, to a bigger, bolder business. The concept of matching brands to consumers has since been morphed into a new, highly successful and thriving proposition of a "pay with attention" advertising business called Genesis Media that is rapidly expanding around video content. However, the remnants of the matching concept will one day thrive in businesses that can increasingly gather data, especially as mobile becomes more personal and prevalent in the lives of more human beings.

BE TRANSPARENT

Transparency is often the key to trust. My recommendation is tell consumers what you want, why you want it, and what you'll do with it. Be clear that you may resell their information for their benefit. The more you share data about them, the more you should "thank" them. Thanks can come in many forms. Your company is likely benefiting financially from the sale or reuse of consumer data. It's time to both share the fact that you are using consumer data and the financial upside in whatever form you choose to deliver this back to your loyal consumers. Sadly, I think there are very few examples of companies that are aggressively transparent about their data capture and use practices as well as providing an ongoing value exchange.

REWARD DATA SHARING

Reward your consumers for sharing both voluntary and involuntary information. The more they do, the more you reward. Rewards can come in monetary form, deeper discounts, loyalty points, and more. Reward submissions generously and update it often with further rewards for each activation. You will find quickly that your data is more robust, up to date, and valuable. Be generous and the consumer will be generous with you.

GIVE AWAY A LOT TO GET EVEN MORE (DATA)

Martha Stewart impressed me with one piece of advice to us cooking enthusiasts: "Buy the best you can afford." Whether honey, bread, wine, duck pâté, or eggs, the differences are probably subtle at best and non-differential at worst, especially for the most expensive brands.

I carry this advice forward to you. Organize promotions, giveaways, and deeper discounts to get more voluntary information. Nothing beats a good contest. In our TV business, we see 20 to 30 times the activity on Facebook and Twitter when we post a giveaway. It could be anything from a $500 woman's leather jacket to a $5,000 cruise for two. You would be amazed at the information people will give up for a chance to win. Always give away something meaningful—make it painful for your business to get better voluntary information. It's only short term. The long-term gain of the data will change the complexion of your business and business decisions.

BE NICE

My mother still says, "You catch more flies with honey than vinegar." This couldn't be truer when it comes to collecting data. If you befriend your customers, then your customers will share more, increasing your voluntary data quotient. I think Starbucks has actually turned niceness into a fine art. The baristas are friendly and engaging as well as damn good coffee drink creators. They know people by first name, know their drinks, their occupations, and more. This data will never be collected in a database, but is instead useful for on-the-ground field research. Finding out what's working or not is as easy as calling a few stores and receiving immediate, genuine reactions to new products, growing tastes, and changing economics and interests. Being nice has catapulted Starbucks into having the most voluntary data in the world.

BE ETHICAL

You've heard the religious saying, "Do unto others as you would have done unto you." Don't use your consumers' data in ways you wouldn't want other brands to use yours.

I urge every marketer out there to consider the kind of information you are capturing and leveraging. Sharing and selling this data may help close quarterly profits, but it will also taint your relationship with the consumer. Just like the commandment, "Thou shall not steal," we have to think of identity information as personal property. Just because it's intangible doesn't mean it has zero value. In fact, intangible voluntary data is probably the most valuable of all properties. It's what you own about your identity. Just like it's illegal to steal money from another's banking account, it's wrong to misuse the personal identity information of that same person. Unless, of course, you are transparent and seek permission, you must be respectful and ardent about preserving people's rights to privacy when making decisions on how to use their data.

While the idea of data can conjure up all kinds of thoughts, fears, and opportunities, there has never been a more exciting time to gather data, leverage information, and communicate to customers via mobile. If we stay true to a few principles, we will get more data than we can ever use and appeal to those most likely to buy.

CHAPTER 11: THUMB'S UP TIPS

- The simple rule of thumb is, treat your customers how you would like to be treated by other brands.

- Work hard to get customers to volunteer data—especially about their mobile device, as voluntary data is always more valuable than involuntary data.

- Capture and use of data—especially over mobile devices—is about more than consumer protection, it's about trust and delivering more value in return for the data they volunteer.

CHAPTER 12

The New Chief Mobile Officer

I WANT TO LOOK FORWARD AND TALK ABOUT how modern business marketing needs to reshape its thinking, training, planning, and organizing in the face of mobile advancement. It's both the easiest and most difficult chapter to write. It's very easy for me to coach and cheerlead the marketing industry toward positive change in the mobile space. As a business owner with my own brands deeply rooted in traditional media, I struggle and strive every day to think about how mobile can enhance these businesses. At the same time, I want this chapter to be my homage of sorts to the industry. It's my love letter to an industry that has made me love marketing and has shaped who I am, how I think, and what my vision is in light of a new mobile era. Please indulge me as I present my perspective on how business needs to evolve marketing.

Without question, you now know that I and others who have contributed to this book believe that mobile is soon going to be the primary platform for every human on the planet. Why? Distribution—largely advanced and enabled by portable devices—becomes much easier for forms of communication, like video, that have until now taken up significant bandwidth. As a result, mobile forms of communication are going to evolve, from voice and the written word to video. As such, the business mind-set has to change completely for this future to happen successfully.

The first change that needs to happen is a reconfiguring of how organizations are structured in light of mobile technology. Most of you will agree with this notion for a variety of reasons, but many of us also know it's foolhardy to try for such massive organizational restructuring that's sorely needed across business. So, let's start small and with those eager to make themselves an example of change for the rest of their company. Let's start with the executive officers. Titles, and as a result, functions in the corporate suite of officers have not really changed in my lifetime. For as long as I can remember, there's been a Chief Executive Officer, Chief Operating Officer, Chief Financial Officer, Chief Marketing Officer, and so on. Only in the last two decades have we started to see the Chief Information Officer and, in some cases, the Chief Product Officer get seats at the table. In large measure, these jobs have simply expanded responsibilities for more budget and power, yet few have sat back and said, "In this era of mobile, are the new responsibilities aligned with the right functions and, more importantly, do we need to create different types of 'Chiefs' both in titles and functions?" Not seeing more re-thinking of the executive suite is really surprising given the globalization of business, the rapid expansion of mobile technology, and the amazing evolution of the global consumer.

So, in the spirit of starting small, I propose and predict that we will see the first widely visible expansion in the executive suite—the new Chief Mobile Officer or, as I have coined it, "CoMo" (Chief of Mobile). Why? With the proliferation of mobile and its impact, we need someone providing mobile guidance, knowledge, best practices, and investment to every aspect of the business, especially and starting with marketing, activating advertising, and then moving to impacts on operations, inventory, and more. The scale of mobile and its importance to business will be reasons for companies to carve out a mobile function, invest in resources, and create a leadership position that ensures the company is operating at the highest possible level on the mobile platform. A Chief Mobile Officer function added to the executive suite puts the platform front and center as the mobile conscience of the company. While certainly mobile functions and responsibilities will reside within functions such as finance, marketing, and product development, having a centralized leader will ensure advancement and cooperation, eliminate duplication, and maximize investment.

When you stop to think about it, adding the Chief Mobile Officer really can help an entire enterprise keep up with the lightning-fast advancements in technology, software, applications, process improvements, consumer adoption of new mobile features, and more. All of the principles presented in *All Thumbs* really require a full-time function to ensure that the different parts of the company are working together, budgets are not being duplicated, technologies have proper security, and training is happening at every level. In some instances, we are starting to see similar functions emerging along with the pain points that will prompt the evolution of a Chief Mobile Officer.

Carolyn Everson told me that Facebook recently put its engineering teams through extensive mobile training. "Mobile development is so critical to our future that Mark Zuckerberg put in place an initiative to train our coders and engineers in mobile. Over the last 18 months, our coders and engineers have gone through extensive training."

Wendy Clark at Coca-Cola is another trailblazer who could easily become her company's next Chief Mobile Officer. Every day she is working with her teams to build marketing efforts for the world's most iconic and well-known brands. She pushes the different brand teams to develop mobile activation with every campaign in an impressive way.

Clark points to Facebook, as it represents one new "ladder" to climb to the future: "Facebook is a good analogy to mobile. It's just not comparable to the media that got us to this point. It's the largest platform with the most engagement of any media I can name with 50 percent of its base visiting every day. Mobile is similar in terms of engagement. As long as advertisers put mobile through the same existing [media] paradigm and structures, then it will only be an afterthought. And yet, if I look at my core target being teens and young adults, it's the most important medium I can use."

Procter & Gamble is a leader in more ways than one and seems to get mobile. Mark Pritchard, its Chief Marketing Officer, is also becoming its de facto Chief Mobile Officer. I saw firsthand P&G's use of Shazam for the 2012 Olympics and now see them regularly create mobile activation of standard print ads. P&G seems to understand that every piece of creative needs to contain a mobile experience. In fact, every executive I spoke with always highlighted that P&G is the leader on the mobile front and is the one to take cues from on how to build for this mobile future.

While this may not be the case at P&G, elsewhere mobile still takes a backseat to the primary efforts in building a marketing campaign and running a business. With mobile devices becoming the largest growing platform ever to exist, we have to start to rigorously set the functions and budgets as well as look forward with multi-year plans to capture the opportunities before competitors do. If your company is small, take the opportunity to focus on mobile. If it is large, seek to align with the growing mobile initiatives.

The next area of focus to move our companies forward is raising the "mobile IQ." I've found a staggering lack of understanding of the mobile platform in this modern marketing era. What makes it even worse is that we are all experts on our mobile devices from a consumer perspective. I am surprised how skeptical some are of advancing mobile technologies, and how little vision they have on incorporating mobile devices into a consumer experience—even though many of these people constantly look at their phones while meeting with me. However, we have to keep in mind that Apple didn't introduce the iPhone that long ago in 2007, an event that really helped spur the entire smartphone market. But people tend to be slow to react and simply want to follow leaders who either have the financial resources or the guts to take chances, make mistakes, and perfect the problems.

David Sable said this about how he's transforming his organization: "Because there is such incredible technology at our fingertips today, marketers make the mistake of using it as a bell or whistle, a flourish to make something 'timely.' In truth, the core of our business is creativity, storytelling. But it must be balanced with innovation, which drives stories through the right channels. So we are training people today to understand they need both and that it's critical to make sure that innovation is part of the entire process, an integral part of the idea rather than an add-on to production."

SET A MOBILE PLAN

Whether under the guidance of an official Chief Mobile Officer or the direction of the Chief Executive, companies must start setting a mobile plan right now for operations and marketing. They must set good old-fashioned goals, strategies, and budgets as components in individual departments before being rolled into a master company plan. As Wendy Clark and I discussed, we need to set Key Performance Learnings within the mobile space. She says it best: "I love the idea of 'learnings.' Advertisers are failing a lot more than frequently in this space right now than we are on other media because it is such a steep learning curve. The parallel to this is TV, when at the beginning there was no Nielsen, panels, or household ratings. Part of this is defining and understanding the platform. With mobile, we have to start building our own metrics based on mobile-to-mobile comparisons. So we begin with learnings, and then we get to outcomes, outcomes that are measureable to one another, and finally, measurements."

I can point to various times in my career when business set a defined course before market movements or conditions became the drivers. Mobile is one of these new-era courses. We must endeavor to place special emphasis on how mobile will integrate into our current businesses by asking the strategic questions and setting the goals in our annual planning and budgeting processes. By 2017, when mobile will be hitting its peak, we want to be well ahead of the game. What gets measured gets done.

ASK EVERY DAY AND IN EVERY MEETING, "WHAT'S OUR MOBILE STRATEGY?"

Second only to setting a course is asking this question every day and in every meeting, just like Mark Pritchard and Mark Zuckerberg: "What's our mobile strategy?" Executives must start doing this with their teams to set the expectations and spark the planning and budgeting to deliver. Again, just as exercising every day is critical to maintaining good health, we must be constantly looking out for the mobile activation in every campaign and effort. As Wendy Clark says, "I'd rather see us do less across more platforms than do more activity without mobile, especially given our younger target demographics."

More is more. The more we engage each platform, especially mobile, the more likely we are to have everyday successes. Then, we can share our wins, learn from our failings, and help spread the effectiveness throughout an industry that will change with each technology breakthrough.

Wendy Clark, who targets one of her brands, Coke Zero, to younger men, says this about how Coke approaches marketing strategy in general and mobile specifically: "Given our target, we need to shift the approach completely by asking, 'What are we going to do on mobile?' and then see if we have money to do anything else. It has to be central to everything we do."

TRAIN THE PEOPLE

Some companies just don't have time to figure out mobile. But training staff on mobile marketing and best practices as well as sparking intellectual curiosities has to happen right now. I have heard the "changing the tires on the car while it's driving" analogy countless times in my business career. This is often in reference to beginning a business operation that is not perfect yet, but will have to be tinkered with in motion. Mobile represents this analogy and renews it all over again. Companies—large and small—have to be constantly educating themselves on what's possible in marketing over mobile, and then they have to take the steps to learn, apply, and adapt. Carolyn Everson also highlights: "Excellent creative experiences—especially on mobile— have never been more important. We created a 'creative council' with the top agencies to share best practices, celebrate great executions, and train staff members in the keys to good mobile design and experiences."

Wendy Clark says this about re-engineering our market- ing people who were all trained and climbed the ladder through traditional media: "First, it has to be a stance on mobile from the corporate leadership. In times of change, leaders lead. Joe [Tripodi], our CMO, is taking a strong stance on mobile. Next, you have to spend a lot of time on shifting capabilities and creating a community that shares [mobile] best practices, shares learnings, and yes, shares failures—which we still have. And, finally, you have to inspect what you expect. We have to start measuring our mobile investment and creating incentives for mobile. Then, we can start to see the shift to mobile we want."

MOBILE MAKES THE CRAFT OF MARKETING HARDER, NOT EASIER

However, in my experience training has to go beyond mobile. In some ways I look at the marketing and advertising sector, and I see it somewhat devoid of deep marketing and advertising expertise. We have become soft in our thinking or reliant on great creative or superior technology to still develop marketing ideas that sell. Agencies and brands that only bank on awards to showcase their marketing prowess will fall by the wayside in the mobile era.

Never before have we seen a more personalized platform than mobile for brands to connect with consumers. While I have been focusing on the promise of the future of mobile and how the world will change, we must also return to the roots of the basic principles of marketing. What actually shocks me the most as I move from business to business and project to project is the lack of marketing acumen of basic principles. We shouldn't be confusing great creative with sales results, nor confusing a tagline for a brand promise.

And we certainly shouldn't overstep communication bounds when talking to consumers on their mobile devices, whether by pushing messages to them via text or if they pull in your brand experience by activating a 30-second TV spot on Shazam.

Carol Kruse says, "Think about how digital and web marketing and creative practices have evolved. We need the same and more energy, development, and best practices for the creative elements of mobile. We need more training, more budgets, and more standards from the governing bodies and from within companies to elevate mobile marketing to its most creative and least disruptive form."

CONSUMER RESEARCH HAS NEVER BEEN MORE CRITICAL

Online research, focus groups, and assessments of each campaign for consumer adoption has never been more critical. Recently, I was touring Time Warner's Media Research facility, which is located in New York City. The team there has taken focus group testing of new media technologies to a whole new level. Marty O'Neill runs the center and tells me that in its recent testing of mobile devices when in use during traditional media, such as 30-second TV spots, incorporation of music in the spot is critical. Music—primarily popular music—gets the viewer's attention, especially those that are diverting attention to other devices like their mobile phone while watching TV. Once captured, the brand can now parlay the attention in a number of ways, including taking action toward purchase on the very thing that was distracting them to begin with, their phones.

While music has always held an emotive spot in decades of TV and radio advertising, it is critical today to invest in the best musical tracks a company can afford. Why? It's simple. Today, viewers are diffused in their focus while watching TV. They will often be using phones, tablets, and laptops all at once while watching TV. Music in a 30-second spot serves to direct the attention of the viewer back to the brand's message. This is the first priority for music use. Then, the ancillary benefit created with music is mobile activation with tools such as Shazam, which are also compelling in the TV space. Shazam started in music detection before easily extending it to music on TV, and then all audio in the TV and radio advertising and other content environments.

Carolyn Everson provides this perspective: "The average U.S. consumer spends over two hours a day on mobile (according to e-marketer in 2013). Every day, more than 500 million people access Facebook on mobile. The consumer is way ahead of us marketers on mobile. There has never been a medium like mobile. It's the most personalized medium consumers have ever had. Facebook completely rebuilt our consumer interface over the last two years on mobile. We had to understand what the consumer experience was. We didn't go there first. The consumer went there first."

While some research findings may not be new, such as the importance of music, learnings now prove that going beyond the once-emotive reactions allows consumers to engage on the mobile devices. Constant testing in the consumer arena will only accelerate the leverage of the power of traditional media and the adoption of new marketing practices with mobile devices.

KEEP YOURSELF INFORMED OF
DAILY DEVELOPMENTS

In the mobile era, keeping yourself informed is the most important piece of advice I can give you. With social, RSS feeds, and other tracking methods, there is absolutely no reason everyone can't stay on top of mobile advancements, creative new uses, and effective marketing. Increasingly, we are seeing organizations adding mobile areas of focus such as IAB and the 4A's. Individual organizations are also popping up to focus only on mobile marketing such as OMMA and others. Becoming involved in local organizations or in local chapters of national organizations is a great way to keep informed, network, and contribute your own successes.

Another great way to keep yourself informed is to monitor your own habits and note them. Unlike many platforms out there, we are all becoming increasingly adept at the mobile device—both in terms of content consumption and content creation. Never in the history of mankind do we have this kind of "mobile literacy" and have the chance to then use it in our everyday business lives. Watching your own habits with your device, those of your children, and people's habits around you can often best indicate marketing success and act as a template for strategies to employ.

I would say one of the most compelling things you can do for yourself and your company is to start networking with other like-minded professionals. If you belong to the local chamber of commerce or business guild, ask them to form small working groups on mobile marketing if one does not exist. I think you will be surprised how many people want to get involved. The very purpose of local business organizations like these is to help their members be more successful business owners. Smaller to mid-sized companies can effectively and efficiently learn from each other as well as make group decisions on the best local mobile marketing solutions to employ both individually as well as for the community. If you are part of a larger company, you may consider reaching out to others, meeting with those who have mobile responsibilities to network and sharing non-confidential ideas, learnings, and visions.

Carolyn Everson points to some examples of companies that we should follow and study for ideas. "The categories of companies who get it are any company that has been launched in the last ten years in the e-commerce space, Direct Response, or is a mobile app, such as Amazon, Gilt, or any of the travel sites. The gaming companies have also recognized the amount of usage of mobile and their apps are central to what they do." Carolyn and I also agreed that P&G is also a first mover and it goes with their history. "P&G led the transition to TV 60 years ago, so it makes sense they are leading the way for mobile. Anheuser-Busch and the larger package goods, retailing, and automotive companies fundamentally know that if the consumer is shifting, they must shift as well. They are all becoming 'omni-channel' marketers."

GOING BEYOND THE "THUMBS" TO SUCCEED IN MOBILE MARKETING

One of the most alarming occurrences in this advancing mobile era has been those who have overtaken mobile operations within their companies simply because they have the word "digital" in their title or function. In my experience, some of these people with brands, agencies, and within their own businesses do not have a clue how to market to consumers via mobile, yet these individuals are the ones opining on and dictating standards, best practices, and visions for their enterprises or clients. In fact, some of my most equally amusing and disturbing conversations have been with people who lead their company's digital marketing efforts or are the beacons within services providers, but who have never created a mobile marketing campaign. Many of these same executives and business owners sit on panels, write blog posts, and develop industry standards while they have never actually rolled up their sleeves, sweated, inspired, created, failed, or succeeded in developing a mobile marketing strategy of any type that I have described in this book.

Why have these individuals been entrusted with such important operations when they have no clue how to run them?

Well, mobile came upon us almost out of nowhere. The mobile technology to market better, extend existing traditional media, and have a personal interaction with the consumer has far outpaced our collective ability to advance marketing, knowledge, and experience with it. People in digital functions were suddenly thrust—either by their own hand or by those to whom they report—into the mobile world and cast as immediate experts. Mobile is not the digital that we have all come to know.

It really requires that those now given this amazing opportunity take responsibility and get their hands dirty by becoming directly involved in the tactical execution of mobile objectives they set for their companies, mobile technologies they recommend, and mobile strategies they approve to execute. These digital leaders need to fail, learn, and shape mobile success within their companies in order to elevate their own, and their companies' mobile IQ. They need to work from the ground up with consumers who are mobile savvy, as well as with bold mobile thinkers and doers—regardless of age or title—within their own companies who could easily qualify for the Chief Mobile Officer position. It's about learning—not just preaching old and ill-fitting digital strategies for a completely new platform. It's about a dedication to understanding the mobile platform regardless of where it's housed, reported, or placed in the P&L.

All Thumbs does not just describe a new way of mobile marketing, creating an extension of traditional media, or even identifying how consumers navigate their mobile screens. *All Thumbs* is meant to be a rallying cry for those like me who started relatively recently in the mobile marketing, architecting, and designing space to tap in to our inner marketer and focus on mobile as the most exciting advancement in all of consumerism. While *All Thumbs* may be the first and most rudimentary dissertation on the dawning mobile marketing age, I know it will certainly not be the last. I expect that those of you creating, expanding, and contributing to this amazing future of mobile business, communications, and marketing will quickly usurp it.

Please keep feeding innovation for me to share. Visit allthumbsbook.com to submit your ideas, your own mobile marketing accomplishments and your favorite examples of brands that are advancing mobile marketing. I will compile and share then in future editions of this book as well as my other movements around the industry. I look forward to *All Thumbs* being the beginning of the beginning, and to learning from all of you.

Thumbs up to you and your endeavors.

INDEX